SPEAK UP &
BE FREE!

**Breaking the
Barriers of Family,
Cultural & Religious
Traditions**

NAFANUA F. MANNS

SPEAK UP & BE FREE!
Breaking Barriers of Family, Cultural & Religious Traditions

Nafanua Manns
nfmanns@gmail.com

ISBN: 978-1-949826-26-5
Printed in the USA.
All rights reserved

Published by: EAGLES GLOBAL BOOKS | Frisco, Texas
Cover & interior designed by DestinedToPublish.com | (773) 783-2981

Dedication

I dedicate this book to my grandmother Aitogi,
my mother Fogaolo,
my late sisters Tala'iga, Salumalo, Tofa'aga,
my daughters Kerissa and Kahrynn
and all of my nieces.

Nafanua Manns

Acknowledgments

I can't forget those who have helped me through this journey. First and foremost, I want to thank God for the opportunity He has provided for me to be able to pen this book. I want to thank my husband Kenneth Manns for his constant support as I race to meet deadlines and meetings for the book, as well as my girls for standing beside me, helping, praying and supporting me during this process.

I want to thank my sister from another mister, a great friend, Ella Wallace Robinson, for her continuous support, prayers and encouragement for me to move forward with the book. I also want to thank sis Evelyn Vaitautolu Langford and her husband Dave for their support in being another set of eyes to comb over the manuscript, and also Evelyn for connecting me with Faaalu Faletoese Iuli (Alu). In that connection came a beautiful relationship that was forged in just a short time, with the opportunity to partnership and work with Alu of the ICAN Strong Families and Window of Hope (WOH) organizations. That connection led to others, giving me the opportunity to share my story and talk about my book in the Pacific Island Knowledge 2 Action Resources (PIK2AR) women's group chat. Thank you to Susi Feltch-Malohifo'ou of PIK2AR for the opportunity and the platform to share, encourage and be encouraged as well. I also want to thank and acknowledge Maafu Tu'itonga Suliafu of Pasifika Enriching Art of Utah (PEAU) for his story, which to me was even more extreme than mine. Seeing his passion to reach out and his willingness to be transparent so that others can come forth and start their healing process is very encouraging. I look forward to seeing your story in a book as well. I want to thank these sisters-in-Christ whose support for the Women of Purpose Group I am thankful for and appreciate: Ilonka McCurdy, Juanita Rivera, Marlyn Davis and Florence Silita'i (TX); Tepora Beckman (NC); my cousin So'otaga Utu-Terrado and niece May Agae-Fusi (WA). And last but definitely not least are these three sisters who linked arms with me in the beginning and through the duration of the Women of Purpose ministry: evangelist and author Dr. Evelyn Murray Drayton (SC) of Soul Winner Ministries and host of the Tell Somebody radio program, Pastor Eileen Silao (TX) of the Body of Christ Outreach Center and Darnett (Donna) Ebert (TX). These women have labored with me for five years in the Women of Purpose group ministry and continue to encourage me as God moves me to another mission.

May God's wisdom, favor and grace surround and work through me, my family and the mission that He has given me through this book. May all the glory and honor belong to God Almighty, amen. "Weeping may endure for a night, but joy comes in the morning" (Psalm 30:5).

Contents

Nafanua Manns

INTRODUCTION
My Intentions and Purpose

The purpose of this book is to shed light on the sexual assault/ abuse (SA) and sexual violence (SV) problem that has plagued my family and my people for generations, especially women. So, what's new – that's every culture, right? Maybe, but I would like to address my own culture. The traditions, religion, the matai system and the family fabric have downplayed the importance of this problem, and it's more prevalent and damaging than ever in my culture, within my people and my family. A 2019 article in *The Guardian* described this problem:

> Samoa is a small Polynesian country located in the western Pacific Ocean. Fields of taro flank the side of the country's few roads, and coconut palms and ginger flowers dot well-tended villages, where the people by and large live very traditional lives; defined by church, subsistence farming, and loyalty to family. But the beauty of this verdant tropical paradise conceals a dark secret: one of the highest rates of family and sexual violence in the world.

> Last year, Samoa became the first Pacific Island country to conduct a national public inquiry into family violence. Published in late 2018, the findings revealed an "epidemic" of violence and sexual abuse. The report found that "violence is affecting almost all families in Samoa," with 9 out of 10 respondents reporting abuse occurring regularly within the home. About 60% of women have experienced

intimate partner violence, and 20% of women reported being raped, while cases of incest were around 10%. As with all self-reported statistics, the actual numbers are thought to be far higher. "The government's lack of commitment and approach through inadequate allocation of resources, support and lack of coordination sends to people a message that gender inequality and family violence is acceptable," the report found.[1]

This beautiful country with swaying palm trees and white sandy beaches and hillsides lined with taro plants, yet covered with an epidemic of violence and sexual abuse. This sounds sad, and it is – it's very sad. The "selfless community" way of life is strongly connected to a sense of loyalty to family that takes priority over the individual's emotional needs. The family name must be protected at all costs, even over someone's life and health. What is considered legit and what is not is determined by the leaders in the family, in the community and even in the country. The fa'asamoa way of life – ole fa'aaloalo – respect, which is tied to the matai system, must be maintained and preserved. Men with matai titles and positions are the decision makers and the voices for the family and village. This title qualifies them to be candidates for congress. The understanding or frame of mind is that men are the leaders of the family and what they say is law, literally.

However, the family and community can still work together without the abuse and assault. The misinterpretation of the Bible, and the lack of understanding of what scripture really says about each member's role in a family, has tinted and covered the nation, the communities, the church and the culture in a blanket of lies, deception and fraud. We can continue to go throughout our day pretending there's nothing wrong and pointing fingers at those who could be hurting. We accuse, slander, label and group the victims within what we see as appropriate with no consideration for the individual. There has to be a line or boundary, and there can be one, if we properly use the truth of the Bible as our guide. I have learned over the years that some of the behavioral issues among young people may stem from issues that are not dealt with within the family, and most, if not all, are because of sexual violence. No, it's not a new issue, but it's a massive issue that needs to be addressed.

My story is a voice for the hurting – especially those hurting in silence or those who may be reaching the edge of the cliff or the end of the road, even losing the desire to live. The passion of my heart is to expose the evil and damaging effects of this heinous act of criminal violence which is evil in all angles and influenced by the work of the enemy of our very soul. The hope of this book is that it will shine a light on this and hopefully minimize the occurrence of sexual violence and the number of victims, as well as illuminate a path that can bring change and healing to our people. We know that as long as we are in this world, evil will continue to wreak havoc, so we may never come to a point of eradicating this issue completely, but we can affect it in such a way that we can significantly minimize its effects and still have a beautiful culture.

The effects of sexual abuse, assault and violence are devastating and life threatening. According to the Centers for Disease Control and Prevention (CDC), sexual violence in the United States is common. 1 in 3 women experience sexual violence involving physical contact during their lifetimes. 1 in 3 female rape victims are between the ages of 11 to 17, and 1 in 8 are under the age of 10.[2] In the Pacific realm, the data says that 1 in 5 (18%, or 1.7 million) women have experienced sexual violence.[3] In Australia, 1 in 6 women experience physical or sexual violence after the age of 15, and 1 in 6 are physically or sexually abused before age 15.[4] Studies by the World Health Organization (WHO) found that in Samoa, 20% of women had experienced sexual violence from an intimate partner, and 11% had experienced sexual violence from someone other than an intimate partner.[5] Sexual violence is a real problem in all cultures, but within my Samoan culture, it's an even bigger problem. I pray that real, lasting, strong and firm change will emerge within the family, culture and church, and that this change would flood communities all over the islands, as well as places all around the world.

Knowing the extent of the problem makes it more urgent to pursue any and all solutions to minimize and prevent it. I have also listened to others tell their stories, and it is really devastating, even more so within my own culture. Therefore it is with great anticipation and expectation that I have written this book in order to bring to light an issue that has so often been suppressed and swept under the mat within my culture and people. As you read this book, I'll explain more what I mean and share some ideas that can help those who are speaking up, making waves and taking actions to combat this issue within the Samoan culture and around the world.

Research states that some perpetrators of SA and SV are also victims of it. This doesn't excuse their actions, but it may explain why. As the saying goes, "hurt people hurt people." So, with that being said, I pray this book will also bring healing to a large number of perpetrators and abusers as well. My prayer is that these acts and crimes will be dealt with firmly and promptly with love, grace, humility, understanding and wisdom. Lastly, I pray that this book will enlighten and help the perpetrators and especially the abused, the assaulted and the victims to follow the pathways to recovery, restoration and healing.

WHY NOW?

It is time – time to expose a problem that is often swept under the mat, ignored, frowned on and completely disregarded by many. It is time to step up, be bold, be fearless, be courageous and be heard. It is time to open up conversations and address the issues surrounding sexual abuse, assault and violence, as well as other related issues that have plagued our people, our families, our nations and our churches for so long. It is time to speak up and be free. As I write this book, I trust that God will use it to change the hearts and minds of all of those involved, as well as those in leadership positions who can make changes to bring awareness and honest, lasting solutions to these problems. May God use this book to change many lives for the better.

WHY ME?

I don't know where this will go, but I trust that God has a plan, and so I move forward with the heart to do His will and to help others. For the past five years, God has been tugging at my heart to move forward with this undertaking. It was brought to my attention more than once in one form or another. So, here it is. May God receive honor and glory for the lives that will be changed and saved because of this book. As I have learned over my life and reaffirmed through scripture, obedience is always better than sacrifice.

I can't tell you why me, maybe the reason will surface later – only God knows. Maybe this is one of the reasons why I was born and have survived this long. As I have learned in my walk and life as a Christian over the years, we must learn and grow in order to progress to the next level. We learn to go from test to test and from glory to glory. Throughout our tests, God will guide and direct us, because eventually, the test we go through will be the testimony we need to tell and share to help others along their own journeys.

Our story and testimony is not for us to keep, but to share so that others may be set free from the same situation we walked through. I believe it is time for me to share my story and testimony for the many who have gone through the same valley I once passed through, or who are in that valley now. Am I spiritually mature and mentally prepared to move forward with this book? When does anyone know they are prepared? I believe when you have the passion to do something about an issue that is near and dear to you, or to pursue a solution to a problem that tears at your heart, you just muster up the courage and do it. Having the peace to move forward with this difficult task is very important. I thank God that He has brought me to a point where I can confidently and without reserve or hesitation share my story. I believe now is the opportune time. Why? I am confident that I am prepared, equipped and renewed now more than ever before. I am convinced that this is the right time to write my story. It's my destiny and my duty to do this.

WHO WILL IT HELP?

When someone is sick, they need healing, right? This means there also have to be solutions and resolutions for healing. According to statistics, 90% of adult rape victims are women and 82% of all juvenile victims are females.[6] These percentages are very high. This book's goal is to help my Samoan sisters and brothers, cousins, nieces and nephews, friends and associates, co-workers, team-mates, neighbors and anyone who has been affected by sexual abuse, assault and violence to overcome and conquer the effects of this abuse. I want to inform those who are affected by this disease, and those who have been part of it, that restoration and healing are possible. We need to share so that others coming behind us on the same path can see and know that God loves them and has NEVER forsaken them. Of course, our heavenly Father did not inflict these pains. We are born into and live in a fallen world, and the enemy of God and man, the devil, is intent on destroying God's creation – the human race. But God has taken my pain and is using it to help others with theirs.

I love Joyce Meyer's book *The Battlefield of the Mind: Winning the Battle in Your Mind*. It changed my life. Here is what she says about our past and bondage: "Our past may explain why we're suffering but we must not use it as an excuse to stay in bondage."[8] Yes, it caused pain, but do not use it as an excuse to remain a prisoner of bondage. You were meant for better and more.

Let me now speak to the victim who may be reluctant or afraid to move forward to freedom, to make a change because of shame, guilt and fear; because of the pressure of tradition and culture. Release and freedom is possible, and you can achieve it, but you have to want it first. It is a life based on forgiveness, love and truth. It will bring peace, clarity and order to your life. Like Joyce Meyer said, "The pathway to freedom begins when we face the problem without making excuses for it."[8]

So when I talk about healing, deliverance and freedom, I am talking about making the decision to break free, to do something, to take action and move forward to a place of healing, of restoration, of victory and of freedom. I am talking about moving forward to a victory walk that will be the soul to your life. I believe that when a person decides to get themselves free from a trap, a bad relationship, an unhappy time in their life, a difficult situation, they will find a way to do it, even if it means sacrificing something else in their lives. It's hard, especially when our minds are bombarded with negative, fearful or shameful thoughts, thoughts that will definitely entrap us in the prisons of our mind – but it is not impossible. Change is possible and attainable. When we begin to talk about change, about real and lasting change, and we take action, then we know we are going somewhere.

My hope and prayer is that this book will educate and encourage women of all ages who have been affected by sexual violence and sexual abuse. Take courage and take a step forward. Lean on God's understanding and trust Him. He will meet you when you take a step towards Him.

Nafanua Manns

CHAPTER 1
It is a Real Problem Today

"People living in the vanity of their own mind not only destroy themselves, but far too often, they bring destruction to others around them."[8]

Is sexual abuse a real problem? Yes, of course. It is a problem that we need to face head-on. It's a like a sore or cut: if you don't take care of it, it will soon rot or get infected. So, we need to clean the wound, apply an antibiotic, cover and change the dressing often and keep an eye on it. So it is with this issue of sexual assault, abuse and violence in our culture. We need to clean it up with forgiveness, admittance, love, compassion and understanding. We also need to change things up and continue to move forward through prayer, talks and conversations.

The American Psychological Association (APA) defines sexual abuse as unwanted sexual activity, with perpetrators using force, making threats or taking advantage of victims who are not able to give consent.[9] The legal definition of sexual assault is any nonconsensual sexual act proscribed by federal, tribal or state law, including when the victim lacks capacity to consent.[10] Sexual violence means that someone forces or manipulates someone else into unwanted sexual activity without their consent.[11] I was sexually abused and sexually assaulted.

Sexual abuse, assault and violence are from the pits of hell. They are influenced by pride, pornography, denial, control, false pretense and adultery, just to name a few. One *major threat* is the exponential growth of pornography and its effect on psychological, relational and social development. "In essence, pornographic 'reality' (an *increasingly normal reality* for millions of men) is a reality devoid of empathetic concern for women."[21]

Sexual abuse and sexual assault have affected so many women, men and children and have ruined many lives. Some have bought into the myth that there are consequences of dressing provocative or not conducting oneself appropriately or that the abuse could not have happen.[17] There are no excuses for sexual abuse and assault. The fact is, "no-one needs to rape someone for sexual satisfaction. Rape is an act of violence and control. It can't be explained away and there are no excuses."[12] No, there is no excuse, none whatsoever. There is no way you can come up with the right "reasons" why these acts happen.

Let's look at what's been done so far. The topic of sex education in school has always brought up heated debates since the early 1900s. There has been much controversy for decades on what to teach, who should teach, the morals of sex education in the classroom and the religious beliefs of the families that attend the school. Over time, we have seen a change in the way sex education is taught in public schools.[13] I was taught in high school about the human anatomy, however in my culture sex is a taboo subject. We gather our assumptions from others, maybe our parents, from family members or people in the community or church, but mostly from our friends and peers. However, in the 1980s, contraceptives were already in discussion.[7]

Today sex education can be more effective than in the past, but there is still more that can be done. It seems to be more of a bandage fix than about getting to the bottom of it. Are we really teaching sex the right way? Why is this important? Perhaps it could help explain why these acts of sexual violence, assault and abuse are not being addressed. Maybe this is why these individuals continue to commit these acts of crime. This is not to excuse these acts but to bring light to another viewpoint and something to think about.

As soon as you mention words that relate to sexual violence, people leave, discount you and start to avoid you. But why? Anything related to sex in my culture is considered a taboo subject, because sex is thought to be bad and evil. This is a misunderstanding of what sex is designed for. While sex is something you don't talk about in my culture, when I was growing up, I would often hear grown women making jokes with sexual overtones during family, church and community events. I didn't really feel comfortable with this subject until I started learning about it.

So, why would sexual abuse be a problem? After all, no one should be having conversations about it – well, no unmarried girl or boy should be asking or talking about it, because we have no knowledge about it, and we're in a place and stage where it isn't considered appropriate for us to know about it. However, attempts at understanding its purpose and confines have been silenced or disregarded, maybe because it was seen as a dirty subject that you shouldn't be thinking about. But what about sexual violence, when should you talk about that? Sexual abuse seems to have been around for generations in my culture, or maybe in all cultures. The culture of silence and shame about sex has also become an excuse not to talk about sexual violence.

In many experiences, including my own, the perpetrator in the public eye presents the image of a "good person" or a "successful leader." But don't be fooled – be watchful and observant so that no one, including you, becomes a victim. Most times, we can be naïve and ignore the signals, but trust me, the perpetrator who has been doing this consistently over time is watching as well. So, be on your guard. Just be wise and be attentive.

How can we make sense of this? We can't. It does not make sense, period. No, the act, the violence, the abuse will never make sense, so the victim is most often behaving in such a way as to validate themselves – looking for love in all the wrong places; for acceptance; for compassion, pity, love and all the other emotional

3

needs we need as people. However, as for me, when I was looking for love in all the wrong places, I ran into other abusers and perpetrators, and if this behavior or lifestyle had continued unnoticed and ignored in my life, these validations could have easily turned into a type of normalcy for me. The same can happen with other victims of sexual violence.

This is why I love this wisdom from Billy Graham. It makes a lot of sense to me. Not that he was an expert; rather, he was a preacher teaching from the Word and the revelation of the word of God. He spoke about having the wrong view of the body and sex. Most say it's our body that is acting and doing these evils, yet he explained that it is not our physical bodies, but the "flesh," which he described as the sin of lust. He went on to explain that "sex is not sin, but the wrong use of sex is sin. Sex which is supposed to be sacred has been perverted and lust came in." He explained that according to God's precepts and word, "there's a difference between the body and the 'flesh,'" and that "sex is sacred and it's protected within the union of marriage, but the world has gone too far and has perverted it."[14] So, outside of the confines of marriage, sex turns into sin, and guilt enters and follows us throughout our lives.

Another point Billy Graham made that stood out to me was about guilt, which he called "one of the greatest psychological problems being faced in the world today."[14] Although he said this years ago, it is still relevant today. Self-condemnation is blaming oneself for something. Guilt and self-condemnation usually go together, and they are both devastating. As a victim of sexual violence, you don't have to feel guilty or feel condemned. You did not do anything wrong. I had guilt for a long time because I joined and left for the military within a week after signing the papers because I was mad at my mom. I used to think that God was punishing me every time I had problems at work or at home. I even felt guilty that maybe I was not dressed or behaving in a way becoming of a young lady. Yes, it's proper to dress and carry ourselves in the highest manner; however, it does not warrant being abused and assaulted.

However, regardless of your understanding or what you have learned over the years, Dr. Graham makes a great point: sexual assault, abuse and violence are a result of the perversion of sex. Don't just take my word for it. Here are some facts about the effects of pornography on women and children from a study conducted for the Violence Against Women Network. Research indicate that women and children are harmed when they are "used in the production of pornography," "have pornography forced on them," "are sexually assaulted by men who use pornography," and are "living in a culture in which pornography reinforces and sexualizes women's subordinate status."[15]

Pornography is part of the problem, interconnected with sexual abuse and violence. Here are some statements about the effects of pornography. The writer, Shane James O'Neill, is talking about pornography and relates to it as "self-abuse." I agree that it is self-abuse, because it will be detrimental not only to us and our relationships, but also to the people we love. What he's alluding to is that pornography is most devastating in the lives of many, especially the women and children who are in that environment, which is very sad and troubling. This is deep and true, and it sheds light on a very serious problem, "soul-fracturing trauma."

> I've experienced sexual abuse and I've sat with too many friends after their own abuse.... Sitting with people as they revisit their sexual abuse is a heart-rending experience – literally, like the heart is being twisted up in a grip of pain.... Sitting with and being around people who have abuse in their past means they have pain in their present, and that can be a "drain" on our own lives. So, we often avoid them and run away from their pain, because we don't know what to do with it. I've done that plenty.... We think that pleasure isn't harming us. We use porn and hooking up as a right, a commodity to consume.... Sex is the greatest physical pleasure two people can know with one another. Sex is a remarkable gift. With it we create covenant and new life. And when sex is abused, it creates soul-fracturing

trauma.... It's hard for me to imagine someone reading this and not wanting to be safe for someone like my friend, as she lay broken and beat. I reckon you want to be safe.... If we can learn to be safe for ourselves then we can begin to be safe for those around us.[16]

When it really comes down to it, it's up to that individual. No one can decide for the other person. Each individual ultimately must decide to do the right thing, the noble thing and the godly thing. A statement from Violence Awareness for Women says this on questions raised about pornography:

People who raise critical questions about pornography and the sex industry often are accused of being prudish, anti-sex, or repressive, but just the opposite is true. Such questions are crucial not only to the struggle to end sexual and domestic violence, but also to the task of building a healthy sexual culture.[14]

Whenever we bring up questions or concerns about any subject related to sex, there will be a pushback. I believe people are uncomfortable because it's a widely misunderstood and under-evaluated subject. In that misunderstanding, traditions are birthed disregarding the real truth and intent of sex, and in that context, sex is abused and exploited.

So come with me and hear my story. Walk with me, wear my shoes for a bit, and maybe you can relate. Find out how I coped with the knowledge and effects of the sexual assault that happened to me for years, and how I overcame this, how my story can be your story, and how it can help you overcome hurdles you have been facing for so many years, yet could not deal with or did not know how. Find out how my story can help set you on a path to healing and freedom from bondage. Be released from bondage of the mind and the lies of the enemy, from shame and low self-esteem, from fear, from relationship struggles, whether it's from parent to child, sibling to sibling, boss to worker, wife to husband, or friend to friend. Where ever it's from, be released, my sister, my brother, my child.

CHAPTER 2

My Story - The Beginning

Iwas born and raised in the small village of Amouli on the east side of Tutuila, American Samoa. I lived there for the first twenty-one years of my life and attended school there from the age of five. A year after I graduated from American Samoa Community College. I enlisted and joined the United States Army. After completing basic training and advanced training in Fort Dix, New Jersey, I left and was reassigned to Fort Lewis, Washington, where I met and married the love of my life, Kenneth. We have been doing life together, with the grace of God, for thirty-five years. My family traveled to many places across the United States and some of the countries with the military and we finally retired and settled in Texas, and we have been here since 1992. We have been blessed with two beautiful daughters.

I think it's important to have a place to go to for support and to get fed spiritually. I believe it is also good to have spiritual leaders in your life who are sincere and transparent, and who don't just teach and preach the word but live it as well. My family attended Grace Christian Center for 12 years and then moved to several smaller Samoan churches before we settled at Destiny World Outreach Center in Killeen, Texas, in 2009.

I'm a veteran of the United States Army with twenty-one years, retiring at the rank of Sergeant First Class. I have a BS in Business Administration and a M.Ed. in Instructional Education. For eight years I worked and taught for Killeen and Copperas Cove

Independent School Districts. I founded and facilitate a women's prayer group called Women of Purpose Group, and I am also a part of and currently the Prayer Chair for the Killeen AGLOW Lighthouse and I am also an entrepreneur. Before this book came along, I was actively facilitating the WOP Group prayer meetings, running my business and living and enjoying retired life.

Many leaders of the faith have deposited great wisdom into me and have contributed to my growth and journey through life. God placed them in my path so He can speak to me through them and teach me more about who He is and how He is. Those who have left the most impact in my life include Joyce Meyers, Marilyn Hickey, Kenneth & Gloria Copeland, Creflo Dollar, Oral Roberts, Rod Parsley, Benny Hinn, T.D. Jakes, Billy Graham, Paula White, John Hagee, Pastors Terry & Jan Whitley, Reinhard Bonnke, Pastor Siaosi Mageo, Pastors Chad & Marla Rowe, Chuck Pierce, Cindy Trimm, Jan & Paul Crouch, David & Debbie Katina, Joseph Prince and Myles Monroe. Others who have mentored me as well through their teachings are Napoleon Hill, Darren Hardy, Les Brown, Zig Ziglar, Eric Worre and Robert Kiyosaki.

There are many others in my extended family and in the church community who have influenced my life. Ta'afua Tauiliili, my childhood pastor and my first spiritual father, was well respected by my parents and the village. He was firm and straight to the point. Parents in the church also supported the pastor's discipline measures. I feared him but looked up to him. When he spoke, I listened. I always talk about how he was a great pastor and leader for our church and village. Abraham (Abe) Malae is a cousin of mine, but one of the grown-ups in my family. In my culture, we refer to grown-ups as uncle or aunt. He would ask me and my friend Tele questions about our plans for the future, and then he would encourage us to go for it. At the time, he had a bachelor's in Chemistry and Civil Engineering. He helped me focus on what I could do and be better at when I got older. He asked about what subjects were my favorite, and used that to narrow my field of goals to aim for as I finished school and headed into the world of opportunities. This is the main thing that guided my decisions in the military. A few years later, he spearheaded the American Samoa Power Authority (ASPA), the first contracted power company in American Samoa. He was also selected as the Chief (Utu) of my extended family. Later, he was selected as a candidate for governor of American Samoa.

My aunty Fuatai Tyrell is my favorite aunty. Yes, I am going to play favorites, and it's okay! She's my favorite because she always gives me life-changing advice, whether I want it or not. She's always looking to give guidance that she believes will best serve me and the family as a whole. She is the matriarch of the family and when she speaks, everyone listens. She is the oldest of the girls, and second oldest of my dad's siblings on the Tuialu'ulu'u side. I always like visiting her when I get the chance because she's not afraid to speak her mind. As she got older, her demeanor and opinions somewhat softened towards religion and cultural influence. Instead of telling me that I should be in one specific church, she started advising me to stay faithful and to continue to pray.

My uncles Tua Falemanu and Auvasa Lavea'i Tala'i are my dad's brothers on the Utu side. They were our fathers when my dad died. They were a constant presence in our gathering and in our lives. Uncle Tua had a strong presence and was well respected and looked upon by many, including my family, his dad's family and people he worked and did business with. He would have made a great politician. One thing I love and remember about him was that he would never say "no" or turn me away when I would show up at his office to ask for bus fare or lunch money during my college years. I used to be afraid of him. He was very tall and had a strong personality. I admire and remember how successful he was in his job with the government and a leader for our family. He also encouraged me to be successful.

My uncle Tala'i was a more subtle and quiet encourager. He was the softer side of my uncle Tua. He loved his brother (my dad), and he did all that he could for us. All of them have passed on, including my mom and dad, who have left a great legacy for me and for my family. I miss all of them and will be forever grateful. They each had time and an ear for me.

Although at times we bump heads, my older sister Vai and brother Fatu helped shape who I am today as well. They were a great influence and support in my life. Vai was very helpful in my family. She helped my dad with bills, groceries, and even the family vehicle and house. She was also a big help for me when I was in high school and college. Fatu left home when he was just a sophomore, joined the military, got married and started a family, but he would come home often and was a big influence in my life as well. I remember when he was willing to pay for me to attend private school. I also remember one time he came home, and I had just gotten my license but couldn't drive a stick-shift. He gave me the keys to my sister's truck and told me to just drive. Thank God where I had to drive the truck wasn't far, because I drove that truck in the first gear all the way to where he was! My brother and sister are both a big part of my immediate family. The decisions they make influence much of how we deal with family issues such as funerals and weddings (fa'alavelave), which are big deals within my culture.

My mother was not just my mom but also my teacher. She taught me how to sew, cook, wash clothes and weave mats. The best thing my mom taught me was the importance of prayer. She would wake up at around 5am everyday to pray. It wasn't just her, it was everyone. We had to get up and sing a song and recite one of her favorite scriptures she had memorized. I remember sitting up, still tired and cold, wrapping my "ie afu" cover around me, with a pillow on my lap to support my arms and head. If she noticed you were asleep, she would "oke" scold you. She also conducted prayer in the evenings. Most times, my dad wouldn't get home from work until way after 6pm, which was the time we prayed as a family and for the village. There was a curfew at 6pm for evening prayer and 9pm for everyone to be home, no hanging out on the "malae" open area in the village where games or activities take place.

My dad was the disciplinarian in our home. He was mostly stern with my older brothers. I remember him most as my daddy, who would always give me some money for ice cream, candy and icicles. In his last years of life, I spent a lot of time listening to his "talks" while he ate his meals. He would usually arrive home late, after prayer and meal times, so I was usually the one who served him his meal and waited on him. This was probably my most memorable time with him. I was in high school at the time. I would try to get permission to go to a school activity, and he would say no in a roundabout way. In my last year of high school, I did manage to sneak away to football and softball games. He was not happy about that, but I did graduate with honors.

He was taken away from us too soon. We had many talks – or, should I say, he had many talks with me. I think back to those times and remember his words and advice, and how I appreciate why he gave that advice as well as why he was strict with me when it came to school activities. Life has its ups and downs and can be unpredictable, interesting, painful, sad, fun, satisfying and so on. Just like the saying in the movie *Forrest Gump*, "life is like a box of chocolates: you never know what you're gonna get."

HELLO, UNCLE SAM!

Because my parents couldn't afford to pay for my college, I decided I was going to go out on my own and work and get myself through college. I had finished my two years at the local community college and was having no luck finding a job. In order to get higher education, I would have to move off-island and attend a university. The closest was in Honolulu, Hawaii – however, it didn't quite work out how I had planned. I wanted to move to Honolulu and stay with my aunt, get a job there and attend college. When my mom approached me and ask about considering joining the military to pay for college, I got mad. I felt like it was unfair. But I made the decision that day to visit the recruiting office, and that visit started the process of joining the military the very same day. The military was my next move.

I never had an interest in the military, but it was a way out and off-island for me. There was nothing to do there, as far as I was concerned, and I didn't want to sit around and do nothing. It was hard to get a job. I tried applying for a few and had no luck. Back then, just like today, it was who you know and not what you know. There are only so many jobs for a specified number of people and specialties on my island. However, some people do make it. Those destined to remain and return to our homeland, our islands, will return and can be the positive and productive change for our people, and many do just that. Unfortunately, many do just the opposite as well.

I thank God that even though I rushed into my decision to join the military, it turned out to be a blessing. It's funny how the turn of events leads you down certain paths – but the Almighty was well aware and in fact orchestrated it all. He already knows the end from the beginning. I love my family, yet the demon of abuse is no respecter of persons; it attacks whomever it will to steal, kill and destroy (John 10:10). In fact, I believe it's a curse. That curse has been broken over me and my children. Each mother or father is responsible for ensuring that their children, grandchildren and great-grandchildren are freed from the cords of the curse over his or her family. This will require spiritual wisdom, courage, tenacity and persistence.

THE STRUGGLE

My life as a little girl was fun and memorable. But when the rape started happening at age nine, the little girl quickly grew up. I started staying at my oldest sister's house a lot. At one point, when they moved to a different village, I went and stayed with them. I did this to stay away from my cousin. I wonder sometimes who else fell victim to this same cousin, and it's sad to think that he is not the only cousin who was doing this.

I was sexually exploited by another cousin at four or five years old. Somehow, this was the talk among some of the boys in my family, because I was asked inappropriate questions about this incident by the cousin who later raped me. I remember vividly where and what he asked me. I call that sexual exploitation. I didn't realize that I was being exploited until he raped me.

I was about nine years old when my own cousin raped me, not just once but several times. The rape seemed like it was going on forever, because I was doing everything I could to stay away from him. I literally got to the point where I was disgusted with this individual and could not stand him. Every night when I got ready for bed, I tried to be conscious of where I slept, and I would go to sleep very late so that everyone else was sleep and I could safely move to an inconspicuous location (there were no rooms in the house) and choose a place to sleep where he won't find me. But, yet again, the perpetrator would somehow find me. This was probably the reason why I would go stay with my oldest sister, at my best friend's house, or with my aunt.

I avoided this individual like a curse and a plague. I started despising him so much I couldn't stand him. I was afraid to confront him because he might laugh at me and deny it – or worse, mock and harass me. He knew I knew it was him, and it seemed that he was cocky about it because he was a "good kid" and liked by everyone, so there was no way anyone would believe my story or the "accusations." I spent a lot of time with my oldest sister – to avoid this individual and to keep him from violating me. I thank God for the day he left, because I finally got peace and was free – or so I thought.

I really don't recall how old I was the last time he tried, maybe still nine, or maybe I had turned ten, but I remember I screamed so loud that I woke up my mom, and – typical of a rapist – he ran. My mom woke up and asked me what was wrong. I told her that someone was trying to touch me, although I knew who it was. This last time, my mom asked me what was wrong, and I told her that someone tried to do something to me but they ran out of the door when I screamed. I believe my mom saw him, because shortly after, he was sent to his parents. I was so relieved when he left.

I never told my mom who it was, but I believed she was aware that I knew. To this day, none of my siblings know, and my parents never found out. I did not tell them out of fear. I was ashamed and afraid to say anything or to identify this individual. I was afraid my family wouldn't believe me, that they would blame me. He was much older than me, and it was hard because he was also looked upon as the "good kid" and the "smart kid" by my parents – especially my dad – whom I loved and adored. My fear was that instead of receiving pity for what happened, I would be ridiculed, accused and shunned. I didn't even share this with anyone among my family or friends for years. I eventually started sharing my experience with a trusted sister by chance, and that started the real healing process.

Although this happened to me, I was still a fighter. I remember getting into a fight in elementary school with some of the girls who were bullies. I stood up to them to stand up for my friends and cousins. I consider myself a fighter. I would not let anyone bully me or beat me at academics. It was always a competition with me. I didn't win most of the time, but I came close.

THE CONFUSION

When I was exploited – I will call it that – at age four or five, I didn't realize that it was not supposed to happen. When my mom found out, she spanked and scolded me. I believe because of that, I refrained from telling her what was going on when I was nine, afraid I was going to be scolded once again, and then the whole neighborhood would find out and I would be teased and mocked by my peers. I believe when that incident happened, my mom and aunts probably talked and laughed about it and didn't think much about it after that; however, these boys didn't forget. It was probably like winning a prize to them, so they would brag or boast about it to the other boys even at a young age. I believe that disgusted me the most, when I realized and was suspicious that this perverted incident at a very young age had now grown into rape just a few years later. Do you see how slick the enemy can get? He is a thief!

What's a young nine-year-old girl to do? You're afraid to talk to anyone about it. However, the place where I was raped was at my parents house. What a devastating state to be in. At that age, I'm not sure I knew what to do, other than to avoid being a victim of sexual violence and a victim of shame, ridicule and mocking. I didn't say anything to anyone – mainly because of shame, I think. I didn't want my peers to find out and tease and make fun of me. It was my little secret, and I'm sure the perpetrator liked the fact that I didn't say anything, so he continued. I don't know what he was thinking, but whatever it was, it didn't stop him.

So I went on with life, feeling my way through, moving and adjusting as I saw fit. But in the process of all that I went through, I felt that I was going through life numb, not being sure if I was at fault and wondering if I was the problem every time something goes wrong – at work and at home. At times, I wondered if it was worth going on, or if I should just end it all and free myself from the pain and uncertainty of life. This was life, as it seems. It's like I could not shake it off. Everywhere I turned, everything I did, I was reminded of what happened, or there was something that was holding me back, and I would have to make a decision – should I go this way or that way, should I do this or that? Yes, so is life, you would think, right? Everyone goes through "stuff," some more so than others. But I was hitting a wall with literally every turn I would take. I didn't know if it was me, the circumstances in my life, the people in my life or my job, my home, my family, my marriage, my career, my lack of education or lack of money. All sorts of thoughts and ideas come to mind, because I was only going with what I knew and had been exposed to. Nothing had prepared me for this. Even the people around me, family, friends, teachers, pastors, pastors' wives and many others were the furthest help I wanted. I thought it was just me, but this is a feeling of consensus among abused victims, especially women.

THE STENCH – WHY, GOD?
The stench of shame, dishonor, humiliation, disgrace, embarrassment, low self-esteem, guilt and remorse, worthlessness and being

degraded is a result of the assault and violence in my life. I didn't realize then that the experience left me with this dirty and unclean "garment" that I was carrying around for years. Although I wouldn't let anyone bully me, I didn't like myself. I started dressing like a tomboy because I felt violated, unclean and impure. I didn't feel pretty. I hated myself, because I felt scarred, damaged, ruined and degraded. I thought about running away from home a couple of times, and I even had thoughts of suicide.

I had nightmares all the time when I was young. I would dream of being locked in a glass room, and I'm screaming but no one can hear me. I also had dreams of falling, like falling into an endless abyss, and of being chased by some ugly and nasty-looking beast. In fact, I continued to have these same dreams for a long time, even after I joined the military. I stopped having them when I got the courage, the wisdom and revelation knowledge on how to fight that devil in my dreams. When I fought that devil in my dreams face to face instead of running, I stopped having them. It's crazy, isn't it? It's something that you may have to do if you're having these nightmares. I believe that these dreams stopped when I got serious about nurturing and building my relationship with Jesus Christ and started feeding myself the living word of God.

For a long time, I thought I was the only one this was happening to. Little did I know that it also happened to my sister and some of my nieces. I believe there are others, though I may never know – but then again, this may encourage them to talk about it and release that burden and be free themselves. However, as long as they are silent, no one will know. It is crazy, but it seems like no one wants to address it and fix it. "Let's sweep it to the back and leave it there. Let it stay with the dirt in the corner and forget about it." But the more actions taken, the more voices that speak out, the better chance of minimizing these occurrences. More people will be aware, and many more will be healed, restored and saved.

I know some will question or ask why God, a loving God and an all-powerful God, let that happen to them. I don't know. For me, I don't remember asking why God would allow that ugliness to happen to me. I remember I wasn't mad at God, and I didn't question Him. It may have been because I had switched to survival mode and there was no time to think about that. Nothing else occupied my mind other than finding ways and things to do to survive, to keep that from happening again. I didn't blame God, I blamed the perpetrator.

However, I now know that God is a loving God, that He said that all good things come from Him and that He will never leave nor forsake us. He will be with you even when you make your bed in hell. That's comforting to know – even if you decide to make your bed in hell, God is there. But, of course, the question comes up, "Why did God allow that to happen to me?" I don't know, and I may never know. Maybe in my childhood-mind, God didn't know what was going on, and that I had to do something myself. I didn't know to ask Him for help or to depend on Him. I know this truth now, that the devil prowls around looking for someone he may devour. The enemy knows that each of us has a God-given purpose, and so his main thing is to try and remove us, destroy us even before we make our entry into this world. I believe it's a generational sin and curse that's been in my family for generations. Prayer combined with declaration of God's word over our family is the only way to break that curse.

That's how the enemy works. He will do anything to cloud, block and distort our vision and sight, and if we don't know it, he will get away with it, leaving us blaming God. The devil is actually our enemy, the enemy of our soul. He wants to kill, he wants to steal and he wants to destroy us, God's creation. Yes, I blame the devil for trying to kill and destroy me, not just once, but several times. But as for the perpetrator, no, they can't blame the devil for the wrong decisions they made, because the devil can't make us do anything we ourselves decide to do. We decide those all on our own. This lie of "the devil made me do it" does not work, and it won't excuse the crime and the sin. I'm sorry, but I will not buy that excuse and lie.

Because of "sin" and because we enter this fallen world as sinners, we are surrounded, impacted and greeted with the sinful nature of man daily. This is the truth, not an excuse. It's not an excuse if you choose to do something that is not right, if you let your flesh decide instead of the spirit man in you. The flesh is the sin nature of man. We have to discipline it and subject it to the word of God. We have to subdue and conquer it, or it will conquer us. Because of this, we have to heal and be healed, deliver and be delivered, and free and be set free. We can let our selfish ambition and pride keep us bound in everything sin allows, or we can let Christ come into our hearts and completely deliver and heal us.

MOVING ON
We as victims were not born to hide our issues, especially this one. It is time to enlighten the masses and bring light to this issue so that the victims, a majority of them women, are set free. What's sad is that our culture, the Samoan tradition, does not address this issue well, if at all. Many family, cultural and religious leaders have failed to address it. They tend to sweep this under the mat and be secretive about it. They tend to ignore it, even to the extent of protecting the perpetrator, especially if it's a close relative.

Scripture talks about choosing life or death; choosing prosperity or disaster (Deuteronomy 30:15). God really wants us to live a good life and multiply. He wants to bless us in our lives and in the land we occupy. But we have to do it His way, by his command, decrees and regulations. When we love the Lord our God, we will keep His commands. So our choices are key in a close and intimate walk with God. They are also life-changing acts that will lead you to the path of prosperity or disaster.

I know that He will not give me more than I can handle. I also know that what the enemy meant for harm, He will turn it around for good for me because I love Him. Because we have been empowered by the Almighty to make our own choices, we are left to decide whether to take the left or the right, the road less traveled or the road with a lot of traffic. We are intelligent beings, and no other creation is more privileged than we are. We are designed to know which way is the best way for us and which way is not. We have the sense of knowing, to know what to choose. However, I can tell you that any choice based on your emotions most likely won't be the best one. That's why most of us find ourselves in situations or positions we regret, because we make a lot of emotional decisions. My dear people, choose wisely, and take time to consider before making a rash decision.

Moving on is a decision. I had to decide to move on. If I hadn't moved on, I wouldn't be where I am today. I would probably still be afraid, ashamed and fearful of doing or saying anything that will "rock the boat," so to speak. I may be unhappy and just going through the motions. Or, I may be going from one relationship to another and another and another – or even worse, dead. But praise be to God, for my desire to change was stronger than my fear of moving forward and moving on. I thank God for the courage to just do something and to move on to being the woman He designed me to be. I'm not there yet. I'm still growing and being shaped into the daughter my Father designed and purposed me to be.

The only way to get out of the valley is to start walking. The only way someone will know is when we speak up, when we knock, when we ask and when we seek. When we speak up, someone will hear, and when we knock, the door will be opened to us. When we ask, we get an answer, and when we seek, we will surely find (Matthew 7:8).

BUT GOD – MY FAITH
My faith has enabled me to move forward and be healed. I had to step out of the box and let God lead me, instead of having people lead me in the way they thought I should go. I went against the tradition of religion, culture and even family to choose the path that I felt God was leading me to. Praise God! He is able and willing, and He is faithful – even when we lack faith, He is there, and He is waiting for us to raise our hands and say, "Lord, help me!" He is an awesome and amazing God. Let Him guide you through your

situation. His way is so much better for you and for me. If He made you and me, don't you think He knows what He's doing? Scripture says that His thoughts are higher than our thoughts and His ways are higher than our ways (Isaiah 55:9). He is the same yesterday, today and forever more (Hebrews 13:8). Our Father has the best for each of us. He never changes. What He said He will do, He will do it. His word will not return to Him void (Isaiah 55:11).

What the devil meant for bad, God will turn it around and use it for your good. (Gen 50:20, 45:5). God will use the unhappy, ugly, distasteful, hurtful, painful situation you may find yourself in for your good and for His glory. We see this in the story of Joseph. His brothers threw him in a pit, then sold him to strangers; he was wrongly accused and thrown in prison; but at the end, he was made second in power over Egypt, and God used him to save his people and family. It's a great and encouraging story of how God uses everything to bring us to our destined purpose. So is the story of Jesus. He was ridiculed, ostracized, spit at, beaten and crucified on the cross, but in the end He was rewarded with a seat on the right hand of the Father, Jehovah God. He took on the sin of the world so that all can have and attain the path to eternal life.

Life is short and unpredictable, but it can also be peaceful, joyful and blessed. It is based on our choices, yesterday, today and tomorrow, and if we tap into the right source – that is, God the Father, our Abba Father, our Lord of Lords and King of Kings – life will be easier and our paths a bit clearer and less cluttered.

A RENEWED MIND

After choosing to take that step, it's good and wise to start renewing our mind with the Word of God. Why? We say a lot of things that are really not true, but because we often hear everyone else saying it, we start saying it too. When you hear something over and over and over again, you eventually believe it as truth. For example, we usually hear this saying: "The devil made me do it." That is definitely not true. The devil for years has been putting ideas in our mind that are not conducive to our lives. Ultimately, we have to take control and decide to no longer listen to those thoughts but to make choices based on what God's Word says, on what gives life and not death, on what is honorable and true, what is pure and lovely and of good report, on things that have virtue and are praiseworthy (Philippians 4:8).

It starts with us, by taking the first step to renew our mind with God's life-giving Word. God's Word will replace the old mindset, our old thinking and ways of doing things that we have learned since childhood. "And do not be conformed to this world, but be transformed by the renewing of your mind, that you may prove what is that good and acceptable and perfect will of God" (Romans 12:2). The good and acceptable and perfect will of God – that is what God's Word says about us and what He promises for us, only the best. Just remember, as Joyce Meyer says, "Satan will aggressively fight against the renewal of your mind, but it is vital that you press on and continue to pray and study in this area until you gain measurable victory."[8]

Are we rebelling against God, against His word, His promise? Anything against the word of God is rebellion and disobedience to God and His truth. God also said not to add or take away from His Word – decrees, instructions, statutes and commands (Deuteronomy 4:2, 12:32; Joshua 1:7; Proverbs 30:6; Revelation 22:18-19). He said to meditate on His Word "day and night, that you may observe to do according to all that is written in it" (Joshua 1:8). I knew when I was young that I needed to read my Bible, but most of the time, we were only expected to learn and talk about it in Sunday school or summer school. I don't remember Bible reading being stressed much when I was growing up.

I now know the importance of reading the Bible and how valuable it is to my life. It's something that we have to do all our lives. He also promised that if we do this, we will make our way prosperous and we will have good success. Who doesn't want that? I have seen God's faithfulness in my life as I press in to learn His word, learn about Him and get to know Him personally. If you believe that the

Bible is the infallible, indestructible, ever-living seed of the word of God, than Christ Jesus can help. Jesus said He came that we may have life, and life more abundantly (John 10:10). A life that is abundant in all things. He is the way, the truth and the life. He came, He died and He took our sins upon Himself so that we may have everlasting and abundant life.

If you have Jesus as your Savior, your friend, then we are conquerors – in fact, Apostle Paul said that we are more than conquerors in Christ Jesus (Romans 8:37). I thank God for that. Apostle Paul also confirms this promise in the book of Philippians, telling us that we can do all things through Christ who strengthens us (Philippians 4:13). Not just some things but ALL things. Isn't that great? We serve a loving and faithful God! When He sends His word, it will not return to Him void – that is, without accomplishing what it was sent out to do.

Joyce Meyer, one of my spiritual mentors, wrote a book, *Battlefield of the Mind*, that has become one of my favorites and the one book that opened my eyes to why we do the things we do. It is one of the most influential things I've ever read besides the Bible. This book made a big impact on my life – it changed the way I think and look at things so dramatically. She speaks about how our mind is a battlefield. It is a constant battle between good and evil, light and dark. God ministered to me through Joyce Meyer at this very point in my life, and I thank God for that. This scripture "For the weapons of our warfare are not carnal but mighty in God for pulling down strongholds" (2 Corinthians 10:4) opened my eyes to how the devil works and how I can combat it. Joyce Meyer made me understand what this scripture really means and what it can do for me. She brought attention to it and made it clear, helping me to know how to strengthen my resolve, my spirit man, my mind, and how to defeat the enemy of my soul – the liar, the thief, the destroyer.

The Battlefield of the Mind gave me the understanding that our minds are in a constant battle – a warfare is constantly going on in our mind. Have you ever seen some funny pictures or cartoons of the little red devil and the little angel in white, one on the left shoulder and the other on the right? Our thoughts direct us to either the wrong choice or the right choice. If you don't have a foundation of what's right and life-giving versus what's wrong and brings death and destruction, you need to look no further. The Bible is clear and very detailed in letting us know what's right and what's wrong. The only way to know is to read it and let the Holy Spirit reveal its truth and power to you.

SAVED BY GRACE

This is a story of struggle, pain and victory that I pray will set many free – free from the prison of shame, fear, low self-esteem, hatred, unforgiveness, drugs, abuse, violence and immorality. This prison is a curse, a plague, a disease, a heavy weight and burden to carry all your life. If not addressed, it can lead to depression, low self-esteem, guilt, drugs, alcohol, promiscuity, prison, crime and continued abuse, and on and on and on, this vicious cycle continues. The list of all the effects of sexual abuse, assault and violence is long. For years, I thought only of myself. Why did this have to happen to me? What if I had said something earlier? What if? I was trying to find a reason why this act of violence had happened to me.

I believe the enemy wanted to take me out before I was even born. That's every child, because they are all gifts from God. While my mom was trying to make her way home from the other end of the village during a hurricane, a tree fell on her and pinned her to the ground. It was very close to her due date, and the baby in the oven was me. Miraculously, I was born without any complications or physical impairments. The sexual assault marred and scarred me and most likely influenced some of the decisions I made as a young adult, because shortly after entering the military, I fell victim to sexual assault again, not once but several times. Then, a near-death incident in my late 20s put me in the hospital. I had an allergic reaction to fire ants, and I was hospitalized for four days, swollen from head to toe. This happened when my husband and I were stationed in Fort Polk, Louisiana. I didn't know that I was allergic to the fire ant poison. Normally, the place where I was bit would swell for a day or two and then go away, but this time, I had a very bad reaction. I thank God that He never left me nor forsook me, and that His hand was always on me. He watched over me even though the enemy tried to take me out and take my life.

So, after many years of living a life of ups and downs, disappointments, fear and being on an emotional roller coaster, I finally found peace and healing. The grace of God has cleansed me, straightened my posture and given me confidence and boldness to face life. I found this grace when I gave my life to Christ in 1985. I didn't really know what to do with this newfound grace, and for a couple of years, it was a struggle between decisions to do the right thing or to do what my ego wanted to do, but I praise God He stayed by me. Many years later, the grace of God has not only sustained me but brought me thus far, only by the grace of God. He saved, delivered and set me free from the bonds of sexual immorality, sin and generational curses. Jesus is the answer. He is the only answer. He is my answer. Only He can remove the ugliness of sin, rape, shame, fear and the sense of worthlessness from you.

CHAPTER 3

The Impact of Tradition

THE FAMILY UNIT

Tradition plays a big part in my family, culture and religion. But some of the traditions that have been set and allowed by our ancestors have long been a stumbling block for so many. Let's look at the family unit. In my culture, the parents, the matais eat first, and the children eat last. The father is the breadwinner of the family, and the mother is the homemaker.

My mom was a homemaker. She cooked, sewed, made mats and took care of us children. She was also a nurse assistant at the dispensary in Amouli. My mom only had a 3rd grade education and never finished school. I believe with 11 children, she didn't have time to finish. Yet she didn't need education to sew, cook, and be a nurse assistant. My mom worked a few times, on and off, I believe when the three youngest children – me and my youngest sister and brother – started school. I remember her sewing and weaving mats a lot. Another thing I remember is that she used to make "taupou" outfits from different color leaves and the "avapui." I had a happy and good life when I was very young – four or five years old. I was very close to my mom. She taught me a little about sewing, cooking, weaving Samoan mats (fala papa) and how to fish in shallow water – catch octopus, find sea urchins under the sand and pick out sea cucumbers to eat.

My dad only had an 8th grade education and was a hard-working man. He worked constructions during the construction of the airport and later became a security guard for the local cannery, Van Camp, where he worked for more than 15 years and was eventually promoted to supervisor. He was also the organist and choir director for the church choir. He was a great fisherman and farmer. I used to love going with him when he went fishing with his fishing pole, but I wasn't allowed to go when he took his canoe out or went fishing at night. He would bring so much fish and sometimes he would bring those big mollusks that I like. My dad was normally laid back and quiet; he didn't talk much until he had a few beers. The only thing that wasn't cool about him was that when he got drunk, he would decide to go to the "malae" and chase and scold all the kids he saw and threaten to beat them up. I also remember how he loved to dance when there was "faafiafiaga" from a group that visited my family from Upolu.

At home, everyone had their role in the house. Some of us cooked, did the cleaning, were responsible for dumping the trash, did the laundry or were responsible for the dishes. I did come from a great home. I love my dad and my mom. They were great parents. There were eleven of us, seven girls and four boys, and I was the third from the youngest. I started cooking at the age of eleven or twelve, and I helped my mom with laundry and helped with my two nephews and one niece my parents were taking care of.

Every Sunday, no matter how much or little we had for Sunday dinner, my dad always made sure we fixed some food to take to the pastor and his family, and also our family chief Utu. Upon returning from fishing with a catch, my dad always made sure that the pastor and the family chief and neighboring cousin got some fish as well. My mother was an avid prayer warrior, and she prayed with us every morning and evening. That was the routine – little did I know that those prayers and the life of prayer she led would frame my life. I remembered Psalm 23 (Salamo 23), "O Ieova o lou leoleo mamoe o ia," and Psalm 121 (Salamo 121), "Fa'asaga a'e ou mata i luga o mauga, e ou mai ai lo'u malosi," because we recited them a lot during prayer. My mom would quote those psalms during morning prayers before singing. She would read from the Bible during our 6pm prayer. These were her legacy marks to us, her children. When there were fights between us children, she would always say, "Don't let the sun set on your anger" – "aua ne'i goto le la o e ita pea." I thought, "Wow, my mom has so much wisdom" – she gleaned it from scripture.

THE EXTENDED FAMILY

I have a lot of uncles and aunts. My dad had six brothers and five sisters, and my mom had ten brothers and four sisters. In addition, I had several uncles and aunts that I was close to on both sides of my parents in the second and third generation. Needless to say, I ended up with many first cousins – not counting numerous second, third and fourth cousins from all four sides of my mom and dad's families. My dad had a sister who did not grow up with him. She grew up on another island for years, and they were finally reunited years later when they were both married and had all their children. My mom also grew up separate from some of her siblings for years. I'm glad to be connected now with my mom's sister's children and to have gotten to meet two of my aunts that I have not seen in years before they pass on. The family side I grew up with is my dad's mom's family from Amouli. They say the whole village is related to each other, so there shouldn't be any dating or marriage between the villagers. That, of course, has not remained the same. Nowadays, no one is listening or remembering, let alone honoring that tradition.

Now with our extended family, up to maybe four or five generations, we all live close to each other. Our houses are a stone's throw away – literally. My dad loved his family on both sides of the isle very much, but he was closer to some of his siblings than others, probably because they grew up separately. Only a few of my cousins that I grew up with were like my brothers. (Unfortunately, because of what had happened to me, any brother-like relationship with certain cousins was out of the question for me.) In our culture, once we find out we are related, you are my cousin. I didn't grow up with most of them. I didn't meet some of them until high school, college and when I joined the military.

FAMILY AND CULTURAL TRADITIONS

Traditionally, family as a whole, no matter how many generations there are, is supposed to help and support each other. We are brothers and sisters in a literal sense. I was told stories of how my dad made food for his mom's aunts until they passed on. I would hear my other aunts refer to my dad as their brother. It was the same for my generation when we were growing up. As time passes, and life and other things happen, and as others move off island for school and work, taking their whole families with them, the strength of the bond between the next generations weakened.

In our culture, we have big families. We have our immediate family – mom, dad, sisters and brothers – then we have our first, second, third cousins, uncles, aunties, grandparents, grand uncles, grand aunts and so on as part of the bigger family unit. Although the relationships may seem okay, there always seems to be some strain here and there. What could be the underlying reason for the strain, the stress, the fear, the unsettling feeling, the secrecy and sometimes fights?

Matais are respected, honored and held in high esteem in my culture. The mentality is that we must protect the family name and honor our family members, especially the leaders. Exercising respect in a culture that puts a lot of emphasis on family and the family name as first and foremost in my culture is a beautiful and great thing, but a drawback at the same time. It keeps truth from being brought forth and keeps sin and wrong covered despite the harm or damage it has caused the victim – which is not a one-time impact for the victim but a life-time impact. It feels like you're told to be quiet for the sake of the family and family name, to soldier up, to man up, etc. What good will that do? If it can be addressed and fixed within the family unit, the village, church, etc., why not? Integrity, grace, truth and love can all be used cooperatively to reach a feasible and honorable solution.

With the Bible as our guide and God as our God, we should walk, talk and move as chosen people of God, as godly people of God, and live according to God's precepts, word and will. He is the Judge. One day we will all be judged by what we do and say and how we have lived. I believe this is the reason why some relationships are broken or dead – it is because the trust has been violated and devalued, and it seems to be moving more towards a selfish way of life than a caring way of life. So, when all these secrets and lies surround the family, the incidents are suppressed to keep the "peace," while at some point, sometimes just underneath the surface, there remain animosity, contention and turmoil.

CULTURAL TRADITIONS

In our culture, you don't do or say things that will bring "shame" or embarrassment to the family. In our cultural tradition, it's hard to point fingers, because I felt that if I cried wolf, I would have been viewed as a tattletale, bad girl, big mouth, liar... and the list goes on. I never did, so I can never know how it would have turned out for me, but I've seen others who I know now went through the same thing and maybe even worse, and that affirms my suspicions. But I love my dad, and I know he loved me, and I believe he would have understood and done something about it. I could be wrong, but that was my observation. He loved his wife, his children and his family.

I believe the most damaging cultural tradition when used by offenders is the culture of respect (fa'aaloalo), which is also a sacred and cherished tradition: respect for the elders, leaders and religious leaders. In my culture, we are taught to respect the elders and leaders and to obey them. This may not be bad in itself, but these same traditions have given many perpetrators an excuse to continue their despicable behavior and even ignore, disregard and discredit the seriousness of these crimes and acts. It's in our own personal lives, our family's lives, our church, our community, nation and country. It's within the leadership at all levels: family, church, nation, government, country. Everyone is hiding behind the veil of culture, tradition and religion – everyone, from the youngest to the oldest, student to president, janitor to governor, etc., etc., etc.

CULTURE: THE TRUTH

False appearances damage relationships. The same person you know is molesting and raping you gets dressed up on Sunday morning, puts on their best white outfit and are singing in the choir, are in the youth or are teaching Sunday school. Now, that seems to be the norm. I guess if you want to do or say something, you're seen as being judgmental. Of course, we all have sin – no one is innocent – but the difference is, when you know you're wrong, you at least need to correct your error and try again. But pride keeps most of us from admitting the sin or wrong-doing. This is a problem that has derailed so many lives and turned so many away from the truth.

Children will do what they see the parents do – monkey see, monkey do. I believe when the parent of a child who may have committed these acts has a guilty conscience because they are committing the same types of acts, they will find it hard to discipline their children. They will believe and buy the lies of the enemy, and therefore will not make corrections, or will be afraid to do so, because of what had happened. It's a curse; it's a problem that a lot of us do not realize is ruining our families and our lives. Even worse, those who know about it don't say anything about it. I believe that's where the pastors come in. They should address these issues and attempt to find solutions. However, some pastoral offices are more concerned with their offerings and money coming in, so they don't want to rock the boat.

CULTURE: THE STIGMA

Our culture has put a stigma on sexual abuse, assault and violence. A stigma originating with cultural and religious leaders is now woven within our tradition through the veil of equality, entertainment and mercy bias, as well as the cloak of religion. In our culture and tradition, elders and leaders are held in high esteem. They are the "keepers of secrets or truth," as some refer to them. I admire and value my culture very much, and the elders and leaders were put in place to protect and preserve honorable ways of life for our people. However, those in positions of authority over the years have created traditions that pervert our culture, and they have used their authority to hide the very acts and situations they were meant to counteract instead of resolving the problems for our people and country. It is the people behind the titles, positions and offices who have perverted the culture because of selfish ambition, pride, arrogance, control and greed.

The effect of any efforts towards addressing and minimizing these problems within our culture has been minimal so far, but I believe they are beginning to get attention. Although efforts made to address issues concerning sexual abuse, assault and violence face stigma, bias and resistance in our family, religion and cultural traditions, I know and trust that God will smooth out the edges as this book debuts and other efforts go forth to counter the effects and spread of these diseases. We have to take bold steps to demolish these atrocities.

Are there legal implications of these acts? Yes. Sexual abuse, assault and violence have legal implications. However, even the legal system is tainted and has cultural masks and covers. There are resources, agencies and organizations that are banding together to fight this monstrosity, and also to offer help to those who need it and keep them informed and safe. See the back of this book for a list. It's not complete, but it's a start.

RELIGIOUS TRADITIONS

All the years of my upbringing in church must have helped in a big way, as well as my parents' prayers. Even the times I was sent to serve at the pastor's house every Sunday taught me good basic principles that have helped and guided me throughout my life. I believe my mom wanted me to marry an up-and-coming preacher, I'm sure, but I had no desire to do that. I wanted to be independent. I wanted to leave the island, go to college, get a really good job and make something of my life. I also remember our pastor then. He was strict and very firm. None of the children or youth in the village dared question him or disobey him. You were in summer school whether you wanted to or not, and you'd better learn your line for the play for White Sunday. He was hard on the boys and soft on the girls. I believe he used good disciplinary measures, though those who got the wrath may not agree with me.

In a culture where certain things are taboo, when young and unmarried girls get pregnant, we quickly and secretly send them off somewhere for a little while, to either have an abortion or stay with someone else until they have the child, and then they return months or years later. No, we can't let anyone know because it's the pastor, or she has been recognized and been through the ritual to be eligible to receive the sacrament. We can't look bad, the church can't look bad, the pastor or priest can't look bad and finally the family can't look bad. Looking back, I believe that culture, tradition and even religion have kept many victims from coming forward. For those who did, even the parents tried to hide it, especially if it was a pregnancy out of wedlock – particularly if the father is "unknown" or "undisclosed." So we sweep those under the mat, and we pray that no one will bring it up or say anything. The problem with all of that is the madness, the rape, the assault, the violence continue for days, months and years, even from generation to generation.

Normally, certain actions set the standards for who is deemed to be a good citizen, a good, honorable and respectable person, but people can use these standards to cover up or make excuses for sexual abuse, assault and violence. You must attend church every Sunday. You have to go through the process of being accepted in the church to partake in communion. One must be married before having children. Everyone is family, so everyone knows what must be done – and this type of act could not possibly happen in the family, let alone by closely related family members. We need to hide or make sure that no one knows, and suppress any embarrassing thing or act. For example, abort the baby to get rid of the "problem." In the Samoan culture, pastors are highly respected. We can't say much about our faifeaus (pastors) because they are the leaders of the church. It will cost more to expose or bring to light what has happened because it will cause shame. We stand to lose respect and lose our dignity.

My people are very religious. We love our churches or congregation and our pastors. However, we have moved away from the love and freedom of being released and set free from sin, and towards religiosity. Most are living the good life and having the form of godliness, but denying the power thereof. What do I mean by that? I mean that we have settled and depended on our religious traditions so much that we have lost the main reason or the base of our faith – the power of the gospel and the grace that God has given to us through His Son Jesus. Some would say "we have lost our first love." Have we really? We really have to think about that. The gospel never changed. The gospel is what Jesus came and died on the cross for – for our salvation, to free us from sin and the effects of sin, which is death.

In the community I grew up in, most people attend one of the two churches in the village on Sundays. That's a good thing, that's where everyone should be; however, most are just going through the motions. If there's any rape or incest, you will definitely not hear about it. Adultery is even suppressed, and family members do not want to bring it up. No one talks about it. Of course there's gossip, but that is about the extent of conversations about anything sexual. I saw people sneaking around – is that normal? Boys and girls sneak around late at night. Some of the husbands are cheating on their wives, flirting with and seducing young women, and even some wives are cheating on their husbands. I saw some of the husbands abuse their wives. These men are leaders in the church, families, government and so on. It was a sad and perverted world I saw growing up.

Where is the church in all of this? Nowadays we are scrolling through Facebook and posting scriptures, teaching all day long, but what are we doing? Are we making an impact? Where are we making an impact? Are you and I a stumbling block to your sister, your brother, your spouse, your children, your family, your church? How do we separate legalism from the heart of God? How can we have diarrhea of the mouth about God this and God that, but not lift a finger to support our brother and sister in Christ and give to ministries and charities that will impact lives? Many preach what God says in His Word but don't live it. Then we wonder why there are empty churches and why so many people would rather do something else on Sunday than go to church or listen to a sermon. We're being hypocrites. We see things that are not right, but we remain silent and ignore them. Are we standing in faith, or are we being passive about what people and the enemy are doing? What makes us different from those who are ignorant? What makes us different from those committing the crime?

MY FRIENDS – MY CONFIDANTS

My childhood friend Tele and I were like sisters. We went swimming and running together, baked together, did homework together, and even during high school and college, we were always together. Although she was my best friend and like a sister to me, I couldn't confide in her. I had other friends I made when I started attending high school, and we hung out together and did lots of things together, but not once did I share what happened to me.

After high school, I wanted to go off to college. I wasn't the smartest kid in class, so I didn't get an off-island scholarship, but I did get an on-island scholarship for two years. I got to know and hang out with some of my cousins during my college years, and they never knew. I made more good friends during my time in the military, and I never shared it with any of them. Maybe it wasn't time yet. I have a few very good friends who are like sisters (not many, though), and I don't talk to them as often as I should, but if I call them today, we will pick up where we left off and I know they will be in my corner. None of them knew. When I was a member of Grace Christian Church here in Killeen, I attended the women's retreat, and that was an experience that I will never forget. It was during those retreats that my delivery and healing really took off. I am so thankful for Pastors Terry and Jan Whitley. They were a big part of my life, as well as my children's lives, for 12 years.

CHAPTER 4
Who Else Is Affected?

What about the victim? What about their spirit, their soul, their lives, their children? What can be done? What is there to do? Can someone do something about it? Can we do something about it? When should we do something about it? Should we be concerned about this issue? Who is responsible for implementing the solutions? There are so many questions, and so many of them go unanswered. These are concerns that I'm sure anyone who has been assaulted and abused will share. There are so many unthinkable acts, behaviors and circumstances that go unchallenged, unchanged and ignored. I wonder, how far have we come towards a solution? How far have we come towards addressing these issues? What has been done to minimize and eventually stop these acts? Has it gotten any better – or worse?

CHILDREN

Children are victims. I was victimized at age four and nine. A majority of the assaults occur at or near the victim's home, and a high percentage of victims knew the perpetrators.[(6)] If a child is being molested, raped or sexually exploited and assaulted, they have to trust someone to open up to. How can we as parents, as family, as loved ones help our children feel comfortable to come to us? If the mother is aware but is being abused herself by the father, who is also the perpetrator, can the child trust her? What if the mother doesn't know but suspects what's going on? What if the mother or father doesn't want to recognize it in the interest of not embarrassing the family?

Victims of sexual violence, or any violence for that matter, need to know that they are loved. They must know that with God, Abba Father, they can overcome fear with perfect love. Not only do the victims need to trust us, but our kids must feel safe enough to trust us. I was only nine and didn't want to confide in my parents, older siblings or even my friends. Statistics show that every nine minutes, a child is a victim of sexual assault. Perpetrators are often related to the victim. Victims of child sexual assault are about four times more likely to develop symptoms of drug abuse, and three times more likely to experience a major depressive episode as adults.[6] When I was working at one of the middle schools in Killeen, one that is identified as a low-income campus, I got to see a lot of children with all kinds of issues. With the background I had, I sensed and felt that they may have been dealing with the same sorts of things I had gone through myself.

YOUTH

A majority of child victims are 12-17 years of age, and 66% of them were victims of sexual assault and rape. Among victims under the age of 18, 34% are under the age of 12, and 82% are female. 93% of victims who are minors know the perpetrator.[6] In my teenage years, I took part in small talk between friends and families where others were telling of rape acts and sexual assaults – but only towards boys. Girls, on the other hand, were not liberated or comfortable enough to share any. I know I didn't share my story, even though it happened to me in my childhood and early teen years. For the boys, it seemed like a joke – and so the assault continues. The frame of mind towards these acts was nonchalant. It was a conversation back then, and the individual I was talking to confessed it wasn't them, but they knew of the individual who did the act. It's a shame, isn't it? That's probably what was happening back in my village, even in my own family.

The incident that occurred with me gave me an awareness and a sense of overprotectiveness towards myself. Nothing else happened to me until I joined the U.S. Army. During my first year there, I fell victim to sexual assault and violence again. A naïve island girl, who was a little too trusting, followed a group of girls I thought I had a lot in common with – it turns out I didn't. Following them landed me in a situation I did not like and came to regret. Needless to say, that ended my casual friendship with them. That was not the path I wanted to go down. But thank God, who always protects me.

WOMEN

The percentage of women who are rape victims is pretty high as well. One out of every six American women has been the victim of an attempted or completed rape in her lifetime, and the most astonishing statistics is this: nine out of ten victims of rape (90%) are female.[6] The assault and abuse for most women started in childhood and sadly, it continues further into adulthood. These are high numbers, which shows that little to nothing has been done effectively to eliminate the problem.

In my life, others were impacted as well. I look around now and see the hurt from some of my nieces and nephews, and wonder if the same thing happened to them. Most if not all are afraid or don't trust anyone – even me. I want so badly to help, yet I can only do so much. How can you create a place of trust and safety for them and not get the backlash of rejection, being shunned, disowned, opposed, put down, blocked, sent away, spurned, avoided, rebuffed, brushed off, turned down, resisted, dismissed, and so on, that some have gotten already? Possible long-term effects of adults who were abused as a child are guilt, shame and blame, difficulty with intimacy and relationships and low self-esteem.[6]

SIGNS OF SEXUALLY ABUSED CHILDREN

How do you identify abuse? How would one know whether they or someone they know is being abused? Have you been abused? Do you ever wonder why you're addicted to drugs, alcohol, tobacco? Ever wonder why you wish you were a boy when you were born a girl, or vice-versa? What about dressing provocatively or like a nun? Why did you want to commit suicide? Why did you want to run away from home or not want to go home?

Here are some signs to look for and be aware of in your children and young family members. Are they unsociable? Are they bed-wetters? Are they having a physical reaction such as a skin rash? Are they loners or shy? Are they too cautious or too careless about how they dress or look? Have they changed from a happy-go-lucky person to a quiet and reserved person? Are they too quiet or timid? Do they get mad all the time? Are they suicidal? Are they rebellious? Do they joke a lot? Do they have nightmares? Do they need to be validated continuously? Are they always going to their sister's house or their friend's house? Are they avoiding a specific person? Are they angry all the time? Are they suddenly failing school?

According to RAINN, behavior signs for child sexual abuse are:

- Sexual behavior inappropriate for the age

- Bedwetting or soiling the bed

- Fear of being left alone

- Refusing to remove clothing to bathe

Emotional signs include:

- Excessive talk about sexual topics

- Resuming childhood behaviors such as thumb-sucking

- Nightmares

- Excessive worry or fearfulness

The following are behavior signs in teens who are have been sexually abused. It's good to be aware of these and take the necessary actions to remedy the situation for yourself and your children so that they are not victimized, and if they are, it is recognized and stopped immediately.[6]

- Behavior changes

- Changes in sleep patterns

- Changes in school performance and attendance

- Sudden loss of self-confidence or self-esteem

- Rebellious or defiant behavior

- Attempts to run away

- Suicide attempts

As I learned about these crimes and saw them happening during my military career, I learned that to protect myself, I need to speak up if something I feel will hurt me comes up. I found myself more outspoken – bold, even – and I thank God for the confidence He has instilled in me. If you were abused, assaulted and violated, whether you are a girl, woman, boy or man, there is help. Help is available with many organizations as well as government agencies. This can help you whether you're a believer in Jesus Christ or not, but you should know that God loves you regardless of your race, sex, religion, nationality, intelligence or financial status. God gave His one and only Son so that whoever believes in Him will not die, but have everlasting life (John 3:16). If you want to receive Jesus as your personal savior, there's a prayer in the back of this book.

THE PERVERTED MIND

The perverted and distorted mind, if not disciplined and stopped, will lead to crime, to victimization, to abuse and many other harmful ways. It is sexual perversion. This doesn't only happen to boys, it even happens to grown men. These are some of the early signs of a potential abuser: boasting or bragging, being needy, lying and manipulating, and oversensitivity. Pornography is the root cause of most abuse, assault and violence, as you will see later on. I know the perpetrators know what they're doing is wrong, but they have allowed themselves to succumb to the lust of the flesh. Then there is denial of the truth and refusal to do the right thing. For some abusers and perpetrators, the abuse and the crime continue, even when some think it has been dealt with. Those who have committed the crimes and have not admitted to their mistakes go on to do even more harm to the victims and to others.

CHAPTER 5
Obstacles to Moving Forward

THE PROBLEMS – THE LIVING/SLEEPING SPACE

In my situation, one of the problems that I see was the sleeping arrangement. We had a house, but it was open – no rooms. Everyone had to find their own spot. The kids would normally sleep with the parents. The boys were in one spot and the girls were in another. But what can you do? It was the only available and affordable way to live in those days. I don't blame my parents for their ability to provide a roof over our head. In fact, I didn't mind. It was a home – my home.

Because of this, though, it wasn't safe for anyone. In those days, everyone left their doors open because it was supposed to be safe. In some homes, there were no doors, just a mosquito net. So, is the type of house a real issue? It could be, but not really. It was an opportunity seen by the perpetrators to commit the crime. In my case, the rape was always at night, with me unaware until I was awakened by the assault. What was a nine-year-old to do? Do you scream, pretend to be asleep, or do you hope and pray that someone will wake up and cause the rapist to leave? What's disgusting is that there were one or two occasions where the perpetrator attempted and left when interrupted, but then returned sometime later and succeeded in the assault. This makes me mad. Imagine this happening to other little girls my age, and even younger, after me and even now. Lord, help us. Deliver us from ourselves.

THE SILENCE

I didn't feel comfortable enough to share my story until years later, when I was already in the military. I believe God was pruning me for a set time when I could be brave enough to do so. I didn't realize that so many other women had some form of sexual violence experience. I finally was able to share my experiences with a handful of sisters in the faith. It was such a relief and a weight off my shoulder. God never pushed me and never rushed me. He brought a sister across my path that I was able to share a bit of my story with at the right time. This took place years after the incident that happened to me as a child. When I say it will affect you, it will. But thank God, there is hope, because healing is possible and it is available. Praise God!

For years, women young and old alike have been silent about rape, incest, molestation and abuse in our culture. I believe the main reason why is because the perpetrator is often in the family. It is sad and disheartening to know. So, how can we address this problem civilly? There's always a way; there has to be a way to counter and address all the issues of silence properly.

FEAR

Fear is the main reason that hinders and keeps the victims of sexual violence silent. There are many scriptures that encourage us about fear. The Bible says to fear God and not man. Timothy tells us that "God has not given us a spirit of fear, but of power and of love and of a sound mind" (2 Timothy 1:7). Jesus even said not to fear evil, because "there is nothing covered that will not be revealed, and hidden that will not be known" (Matthew 10:26). God is a just God, and He neither sleeps nor slumbers (Psalm 121:4). He knows and is aware of everything going on with us, our family and in the world. He is omnipresent, omniscient and omnipotent. We should not fear man, because he can only kill the body but not our spirit. We should only fear God, who is able to destroy both soul and body (Matthew 10:28).

The impact of fear to the victim's sharing will definitely have an effect on herself or himself. It happened to me, and I've heard it from other victims as well. Over the years, the incidents have been brushed aside and mainly ignored – the family members who could do something about it do not want to accept that truth. There has been no action taken to help the victims. The victims largely have turned to other options, such as becoming masculine or feminine because they don't trust the opposite sex, and therefore changing his or her entire lifestyle from what God intended for them to have. They have attempted to commit suicide, run away from home, etc., etc. This has been going on for generations, and there has been no clear or workable solution for it.

REJECTIONS

How does one handle rejections? As for me, I learned to tune out people, places and even situations. I pretended it didn't bother me. Shortly after the assault, I got into a lot of fights. I was not going to let anyone bully me, push me around or boss me around. I started to grow this shell around my heart and head, or at least I tried. I started reading a lot. I also decided in my mind that I was going to make something of myself, and it didn't matter how long or what it would take.

Things eased up a little when I started high school. I made some new friends, and things looked promising. But I still had my suspicions and kept my guard up. I learned to tune people out that I didn't care for. I was called a "little Satan" by one of the ladies in the village because I fought with her twin nieces. I didn't give her the satisfaction she was looking for. I ignored her. People are mean and spiteful even towards children – childish and immature.

As time went by, I found that tuning things out didn't work as well as I thought. What I have learned is that I needed to surround myself with the right people and either confront the mean-spirited people with love or just ignored them. It's so much easier said than done. Back then, I didn't know about positive thinking and positive affirmation, let alone how to claim and receive the promises God outlines in His Word for me. So I lived my life as best I could, doing what my dad and mom asked me to do, trying to outdo my cousin next door in all things academics, attending church and helping out at the pastor's house, and enjoying life with my friend Tele and cousins Lanu, Siaki and Fia. These were the people I spent most of my time with growing up.

As I got older, my focus was on school. I went on to community college and finished at the beginning of my third year. After that, there was a lull where I was just sitting at home, unsure of what to do. In the meantime, Tele and I were working out (running and swimming) and were playing around with photography. She was taking care of her grandma Teuila and aunty Lili's children. I think she was just as surprised to see me leave when I joined the military. My parents couldn't send me to school. This is why I ended up in the army.

The military was a whole new life for me. I was thankful that a young lady from Fagatogo, Lani, accompanied me to my basic training; at least there was someone I was familiar with. I actually enjoyed the training. As I look back, I can see that I was covered by prayers. Training was a breeze, and my first duty station was nice – nice friends and people I worked with and associated with. I even met my cousin Tali while at my first duty station. As for rejection, while I didn't experience any as far as the incident was concerned, throughout my military career, there was a lot of rejection from those I worked for or with.

Rejections from family, friends, acquaintances and even the church is not as important if you can stand alone in the courts of heaven when God can say to you at the end of your short life here on earth, "Well done, good and faithful servant" (Matthew 25:23). As Apostle Paul alluded to in the book of Philippians, he had not achieved his goal in life, but he continued to focus and move forward and keep his eyes on the goal, the finish line (Philippians 3:13-14). Paul goes on to say that at the finish line is the heavenly prize, through Christ Jesus.

ADMISSION OR DENIAL

What about admission from the perpetrator? Without admitting to the crime and revealing and accepting the truth, the perpetrator will never be free themselves. Some may think they are okay, but trust me, they are not. They can turn to alcohol to drown the shame, but it will not go away. They themselves may even be in an abusive relationship. I see all of these – you just know. At first, you wonder why all these things are happening, and then when you find out the truth, you put two and two together and realize that this is the real reason behind all the drama. They can deny it or accept it, but it is the real truth.

Since the incident, the perpetrator in my case never apologized or sought me out to apologize. When he visited for a funeral 20 years later, the feelings of disgust and anger rose up again. I couldn't believe he would show up after what he had done. I wasn't sure of the logic there. I avoided him and preferred not to see or speak to him, but here he was. I realized then that I had to do something. I had to heal.

For the perpetrator, they have to admit they have a problem, forgive themselves and seek help. For the victim, we have to admit that this is a serious problem and find ways to deal with it instead of hiding it in the deep recesses of our heart and mind. As victims, having a safe place to go, confiding in the right people, getting the right help, talking about it, forgiving and moving on will bring peace, strength, courage and hope. For me, deliverance through Jesus Christ in ways of prayer has helped. There is counseling available. Go on a retreat with your church and get deliverance and healing. Victims can renew, regroup and restore their mind, heart and spirit. You can renew your mind through self-talk, reading, speaking life into your life, declaring who you are in Christ. Renew your life by taking off the dirty garments (shame, disappointment, fear) and replace them with new, fresh and clean garments (forgiveness, love, sound mind, confidence, compassion). Tell someone you forgive them; encourage and build others like us up.

What about denial? Denial is so devastating for everyone involved. Denial is like the lock to someone's mind, soul and spirit. As long as they are in denial, they will never be able to love freely, live freely, or enjoy the rest of their life. They will be trapped in the prison of their own subconscious mind. Everything they do will be a front, but putting on a front is hard. They will tend to resort to alcohol to deaden or erase the guilt, but it will never go away. Let me say that again: it will never go away.

One of the first steps to healing is confession. We need to confess and own up to the crime or the violence. We cannot circumvent or go around that. Joyce Meyer said it best:

> The truth is always revealed through the Word; but sadly, people don't always accept it. It is a painful process to face our faults and deal with them. Generally speaking, people justify misbehavior. They allow their past and how they were raised to negatively affect the rest of their lives. Our past may explain why we're suffering, but we must not use it as an excuse to stay in bondage... Learn to cast your care, but not your responsibility... The pathway to freedom begins when we face the problem without making excuses for it... People living in the vanity of their own mind not only destroy themselves, but far too often, they bring destruction to others around them.[8]

RELIGION

A religious mindset keeps people from being truthful. There's fear of being labeled "bad" or "sinful." The expectation is to be holy, but people fear being ridiculed, so they hide any acts or incidents that don't line up with God's word and portray a "godly" appearance. There's fear of what the pastor might say, or how the leaders of the church may treat you. There's a mindset that if you go to church every day, join the choir, attend Sunday school, go through the holy communion process and listen to and obey your pastor, you are a good person and you are good with God. All of these are good things to do, but I think the problem is that we do them but don't believe in it ourselves. We do it for other reasons, maybe to put up a front to show others that we love and honor God. However, God doesn't just want our actions and words; He wants our hearts most of all. It doesn't matter what position you hold or how much money you have; if God is not in your heart, we're paddling through life aimlessly. The real reason to do these things is to get to know God more intimately so that you can have a blessed life. So, are you doing what you do to impress people, or are you doing it because you want to please God the Father and honor Him? I hope your intentions are the latter.

RESISTANCE: FAMILY, CULTURAL AND RELIGIOUS TRADITIONS

There's a lot of resistance from the culture, the government, the church and the family. Even now, as soon as someone hears or sees actions taken to combat sexual abuse, they disappear, lie low, stop talking and don't want to be affiliated with the person spearheading those efforts. This is seen in the church and government especially. The most obvious yet most ignored barriers to dealing with sexual violence and assault issues are religious, cultural and family traditions and the stigma and bias they present. It has remained a stumbling block, a barrier, a hiding place for some if not most offenders. Though there may be a lot of resistance from the traditions of culture, family and religion, and from the nation's leaders, I believe that this is the time to bring to the forefront the truth, to shed light into all the dark places in our homes, our villages, our country and nation so that we can address these issues and bring healing to our families and people.

CHAPTER 6

Is It possible to Heal?

Solutions to Moving Forward

W hat is the first and most important thing to do? What about solutions? Will they come forward? Will they want to talk? Will they want to confess, to apologize? Is it feasible? Is it possible?

These are ideas that may or may not work or may already be in place, these are but my suggestions. With God, all things are possible to them that believe. Not just some things, but all. He knows all, and His heart is for each and every one of us to be set free, to live life to the fullest, to enjoy life and to receive blessings and be blessed.

THE SHIFT
It is time to shift our traditions to promote a culture that is based on integrity, respect, honesty, honor, truth and the reverence of Almighty God – the Giver of life, the Creator, the Everlasting, the Almighty and the one and only true God – not just with our words but through real and genuine actions. We must also shift with grace, love and humility so as to move forward with renewed knowledge and wisdom to combat this stronghold of an issue. I truly believe that if leaders in the family, the community, the government and the church step up and do the right things, the government and church will see breakthroughs in many areas, including the lives of family members as well as all of our people.

I know God is faithful and true to His promises. He said that if His people – we, the church – will humble ourselves, turn from our wicked ways, pray and seek His face, He will forgive us and heal our land. This is relevant today as well. He is the same yesterday, today and forever. I believe the change starts in the family, and from there, the church can change and adjust, eventually bringing change and healing to the nation. Easier said than done, but with much prayer and with honest and clear steps, I believe it is possible. These leaders will need to have the courage to make the change, the wisdom to know what to change and how to integrate that change, and last but not least, compassion, integrity and love.

Sexual abuse, assault and violence are definitely not the intentions God has for us. We have to learn to heal, release, forgive, ask for forgiveness and move forward to be able to fulfill God's ultimate and perfect will for each of us. God's way is the best way and the right way. It's lasting, it's the blessed way and it's the only true path to true healing. Before starting any process, I believe there also should be a plan or course of action established so that the healing, recovery and restoration process works out well. Communication must be clear, trusted, private and treated with the utmost care and integrity.

CONNECTING AND COUNSELING

Before any confession, apologies or counseling, information needs to be gathered. Connection to support organizations should be established, and even support from family, friends or confidants if a family member is the perpetrator. A forum for the community and church should be established as well. Counseling and having the right confidant can be tricky and can be an uncertain part of the process. We need to identify individuals within organizations who can be trusted advocates to take the job, such as the pastor, bishop, priests, cardinals, parents or other adult family members. Such individuals cannot always be trusted – no one knows that more than I do – however, we must find the ones who can. They should be present and aware, and also understand that this process is necessary for both parties to move forward and fulfill their God-given destiny. Confidentiality should be assessed when looking for someone to sit in, a person who is trusted to oversee or supervise the process. They must be sympathetic, calm, patient and trustworthy, as well as capable of making the hard decisions to correct the issue.

EARLY SOLUTIONS

A viable and immediate solution could be to separate or remove the perpetrator or the victim from that environment. I also believe some type of redirection or reprimand should take place. It should be appropriate and firm enough to ensure that they will learn their lesson and not commit this crime again. For example: monthly visit with a pastor; attend a class about laws concerning the offense; attend Bible classes on dealing with flesh or on what God says about sin and the consequences of rape, exploitation and incest; no sports or extra-curricular activities.

EDUCATION – RECOVERY CLASSES

People in the community should be educated on the following issues:

- How to deal with being a victim

- What to do if you become a victim

- Who to notify if you become a victim, and when to notify them

- Where to go if you have been victimized

- Signs to look for in a potential perpetrator

- Signs to look for in a victim

- Factors that cause abuse, assault and violence

- Discovering the root cause of sexual violence

SAFE SPACE GROUPS AND AWARENESS EFFORTS

There are groups with weekly discussions on issues related to sexual crime or violence to help victims and others hash it out, so to speak, and get it out in the open. The more you share your story, the better it is for you and for others, because your story is part of your healing, and it can also help someone else heal and be set free. We are not to hold on to our story but to give it away. It is a gift for someone else, to help them and heal them, and in return is the reward of healing for you.

Awareness briefings and storytelling can be weaved into education as part of awareness month activities, like April for Sexual Assault Awareness Month (SAAM), similar to other activities held for raising awareness of an issue.

Education and information classes and websites are also important ways to inform and educate children, teens and adults on sexual abuse, assault and violence ,as well as sex/slave trafficking and trading. The back of this book lists some websites and organizations that can provide information, as well as help you directly or put you in contact with the people who can help you.

How about adding awareness and information as part of the school curriculum? Information such as how to know and identify your boundaries to avoid falling victim to sexual violence. I think it would be a great teaching. We need boundaries in all areas of our lives. Boundaries education teaches everyone, from children to adults, what to look for, what to do, and how to address the episode or occurrence without worrying about backlash or repercussions. Boundaries communicate what's appropriate and how far certain things and actions can go before entering into the no-go zone. "It's important to recognize that healthy boundaries help to protect and respect you; an unhealthy boundary seeks to control or harm someone else."[18] Dr. Henry Cloud and Dr. John Townsend wrote great wisdom about this topic in their book *Boundaries*:

> Boundaries define us. They define what is me and what is not me... Setting boundaries inevitably involves taking responsibility for your choices. You are the one who makes them. You are the one who must live with their consequences... Boundaries help us distinguish our property so that we can take care of it... We need to keep things that will nurture us inside our fences and keep things that will

harm us outside... However, boundaries are not meant to be walls. Instead, we are meant to be in community with one another. But in every community the members have their own space and property.[19]

There are also blogs available that do the same thing as a weekly talk, but in a more discreet manner. Other ways we can help bring awareness to our community are through teacher-parent organization events, radio and TV programs and online programs. It is important to recognize that the perpetrators of sexual abuse, assault and violence need education on boundaries as well, in order to understand how this has been a problem that continues from our past, and how we can address it and move forward with clarity, healing, restoration and renewed and strengthened resolve.

I'm sure these or similar measures have been or are currently being implemented within our own communities, villages or country. Any step towards a feasible and effective solution and plan is a step in the right direction. This will help the victims be aware of those individuals who are or have been perpetrators and lay out preventative measures so that people do not become either a victim or a perpetrator. Initiating the recovery process is the key to restoration. For both victims and restored perpetrators, reassessing and moving forward should be in every step of the healing and restoration process. It is very important. I pray that as we move forward with exposing and bringing healing to our people, communities, churches and families, we are able to live productive and blessed lives and be advocates, movers and shakers to bring lasting and great influence and change.

CHAPTER 7

The Process: Let Go & Let God

The next step in the process should be counseling, followed by a place where confession and apologies are conducted safely and privately, at the proper time, to help both the victim and the perpetrator come to accept it and start moving towards healing. The counselor or confidant should talk it out privately with the individuals involved. Confession is an important action, and the perpetrator admitting the wrong should be the first step. If this does not happen first, it's like standing on one leg – you will be unstable because you are out of balance. The perpetrator must apologize and ask for forgiveness in all sincerity. There is no way around it. Once all of that is done successfully, than I believe the victim can move on with the acceptance of the plea or apology. From here, both parties can move on with life and with freedom – mentally, emotionally and spiritually.

THE IMPACT ON THE ACCUSED

I believe that the accused themselves are not just perpetrators but victims as well. They are victims of their imaginations and of the flesh nature, and they may have been victims of abuse themselves. They will never have peace knowing that they have committed a sex crime; they will try to live their life, but it will always be in the background. The guilt they live with will drive them to violence in their own relationships, whether in marriage, dating, with children or with others. In fact, I believe that because of that guilt, their lives are chaotic, or dependent on alcohol, cigarettes and God knows what else. For the rest of their lives, they will try and forget that it happened, but until they come to term with it and ask for forgiveness, until this is addressed, they will never have peace and freedom. Healing has to take place. They will have to forgive themselves first. God has a purpose and a plan for each and every individual involved, but until this is dealt with, it'll be hard for them to receive peace and restoration.

CLEANSED AND MADE NEW – VICTORY OVER ERROR THROUGH SELF-CONTROL AND SELF-PURIFICATION

We can have "victory over error through self-control and self-purification." What a profound statement made by Billy Graham. He said it and it jumped out at me. It seems pretty self-explanatory, right? These are routes and paths to healing and restoration. What does that mean? To me, it means you can start anew. You can have victory over the error you have done by turning it over to Jesus Christ. It is truly possible. These are some paths you can take to begin your journey to a life of healing, freedom and peace. This is the way to have the peace that surpasses all understanding (Philippians 4:7). God is a faithful God. He will meet you where you're at, and He will guide and direct you as you take that first step.

Paul wrote about our sinful nature. It is something we have to continue to consciously think about and control. Since we now know Jesus and we know the truth is in Him, we must throw off our old sinful nature and our former way of life, "which is corrupted by lust and deception" (Ephesians 4:22). We have to learn the truth, and the truth is in the Bible. So clear are its instructions to having life more abundantly (John 10:10). That's it.

FEAR

Fear has crippled so many. Yet many fail to realize that fear is only from the enemy, and most times it's just a figment of our imagination. As devastating as our enemy intends it to be, fear can be overcome by faith, love, strength, courage and tenacity. Fear keeps most people from opening up in either confessing the sin or releasing the hurt. Fear is not of God. Scripture tells us that "God has not given us a spirit of fear, but of power and of love and of a sound mind" (2 Timothy 1:7). Fear is what kept me from moving forward to a life of freedom and peace. It kept me locked up for years. I didn't know it, but it was taking over my life and controlling it. I was struggling with an inner devil that I couldn't recognize and fight. I was bound with it. I didn't realize that it was the fear of others knowing about it, my family especially – fear of the shame and hurt it could bring.

QUARANTINE YOUR FEARS

During the time when I was writing this book, my pastor preached a message titled "Quarantine Your Fears and Release Your Faith." What a way to coin that phrase, and so in line with this part of the book. We have to face fear every day of our life, and what we need to do is really quarantine our fear and feed our faith, simple as that. Give fear no place in your life. It won't stay if you don't allow it to stay.

Our walk as Christians is a walk of faith. We can learn a lot from Abraham, the Father of Faith. The opposite of fear is faith, and "faith is the substance of things hoped for, the evidence of things not seen" (Hebrews 11:1). So remove fear and embrace faith. As God directed my paths and pulled me through, I learned through my experiences different ways to cope with what I was struggling with. Little did I know that all the fears, shame and guilt I had stemmed mostly from this experience.

GOD'S GRACE

Is it a curse? Is it my fault? Is it my cousin's fault? Is it my parents' fault? Whose fault is it? The world we live in certainly is an evil world, and most times, the enemy is a key influence on these acts of violence – I said most, not all. Often, it's us and our stubbornness, disobedience, pride, arrogance and ignorance. There are women who deny that they are hurting. There are some sisters in the church who deny they have any hurts or pain, insisting that they have forgotten about it and have moved on. But are you really free from the pain of the past? We have built a shell around our heart in that area where we were hurt. We go through life thinking we're okay, but we really need to face it, not only for ourselves, but for our children and for other women. We won't know until something triggers that pain, and then we are having an emotional breakdown. Healing has to take place, my sister, my fellow comrade. Healing has to take place for you to experience real freedom. Praise God for His grace, love and mercy that I have lived to learn and grow from these experiences, and that I can at least reach out to some of you and let you know that I know, and that I was there too.

HOPE AND THE RIGHT CHANGE

It is also good to know that this is not the end, and choosing the wrong lifestyle does not make it go away or erase the hurt and pain you suffered from the experience. You do not have to cut all men or all women out of your life. God has a mate especially for you. You do not have to continue to defile yourself or get into numerous relationships to deaden the pain. You don't even have to be promiscuous, sleep with whomever or feel that you have to degrade yourself. Yes you are degrading yourself – you are worth more than that, and you should be honored and respected for men to like you. We don't need a man or a woman to validate our self-worth.

I believe everyone is destined to a certain mate, designed and orchestrated by the Father, our God. You and I are more than conquerors. We are made in God's image. We are the daughters of the Most High God. You are beautiful just as you are. There is only one of you – no one else has your DNA. You were made and destined for a purpose. You are special, unique and altogether beautiful. There is a saying I hear once in a while, "God don't make no junk," and that's true. If we were made in His image, then we are not ugly, too tall or too short, too skinny or too fat, too big or too small, etc. No, God surely did not make and does not make junk. In fact, He referred to women after He created them to be very good (Genesis 1:31) – inherently and intrinsically good.

FORGIVE

I have to forgive; you have to forgive. I had to forgive myself first before I could forgive the perpetrator. Forgiveness releases you to live free from fear, shame and condemnation. Forgiveness brings salvation to you and your family. Forgiveness releases the victim from their prison of shame, condemnation and self-pity. Forgiveness is the first and most important step in the process. I have forgiven the perpetrator in my case. I don't think I'll ever have a normal relationship with him, but you never know. God uses everything to bring joy, freedom, favor and blessings to us and to bring honor to Himself. He is a merciful and loving God.

When you forgive, you receive power. What does that mean? There's something about forgiving someone – it's mainly for you and not for the other person. There's a hold that the enemy has over you when you walk and live in unforgiveness. It's not healthy, it's not friendly to your life and it's not good for your loved ones, your friends – it's not good for anyone, not even you. Forgive and gain peace. Speak and release to be free from the bondage. Allow God to heal you and gain freedom. The power you receive is the power to be free, to be happy and joyful and to move on with life. Unforgiveness is a curse. It's detrimental to your life as a whole. It will have a hold on your life like a grip. You may be happy, but it won't be for long. You may be successful, but you'll be miserable. You may have all the things you want, but still feel empty. What a disaster! Forgive! Forgive and live life to the fullest. God will not forgive you if you don't forgive others. Let Him worry about them; you just forgive. Do it for yourself.

When you forgive, you must also renew your mind with God's Word. If you don't renew your mind, the enemy will tempt you, harass you and do everything to make your life miserable. Renewing your mind with the Word is so powerful and life-changing. God's promises are the best for everyone. There is no way you will walk through life without the guidance of the scriptures, because they are God-breathed and they are life. God's Word gives life, but only when you do it, not just say it. You have to walk it out. Renewing my mind with the Word of God was another breakthrough revelation that changed me.

I remember the time when I stumbled upon a radio program on my 30-minute commute to work while stationed in Virginia. It was none other than Joyce Meyer, and I started listening to her on the radio every morning as I made my way to work. A few years later, she published *The Battlefield of the Mind*. I bought the book and told myself I would read it, just because the title looked like it would be a great book. Well, when I started reading it, it literally changed my way of thinking. This book changed my life tremendously. It must have been one of those books that God ordains every once in a while to supercharge His people. I have been through so much turmoil and confusion that this book came just at the right time. It really opened my eyes about all the wrong thinking that we grew up with: the labeling, the name calling and all the words that were said to us that were not life-giving. I read the book two or three times because of all the information in it. It helped me overcome doubts, anxiety, fear, condemnation, self-pity and many other types of wrong thinking and ideas about myself. It helped me understand the damage those statements, names and words can do to a child. I thank God for Joyce Meyer and her testimony, as well as the teaching she taught through *The Battlefield of the Mind*.

WHAT'S LOVE GOT TO DO WITH IT?

What is love? "Love is patient and kind. Love is not jealous or boastful or proud or rude. It does not demand its own way. It is not irritable, and it keeps no record of being wronged. It does not rejoice about injustice but rejoices whenever the truth wins out. Love never gives up, never loses faith, is always hopeful, and endures through every circumstance" (1 Corinthians 13:4-7).

Billy Graham said this about love. He said it is "the most misused word in all of the English language," and that it is "misunderstood and misused so much today."[14] Without love, there can be no forgiveness. Without love, there is no hope. Love covers all. Love is what will help us through the valleys until we get to the mountain. But when love is taken out of context of what the Bible meant it to be, it will be misconstrued, misused and abused. The Bible says "perfect love casts out fear" (1 John 4:18). So, with God's perfect love, we can cast out fear and take the path towards our healing through forgiveness.

LET GO AND LET GOD

For victims of sexual violence, know that you are loved. You must know that with God, Abba Father, you can overcome fear with perfect love. Perfect love is God's love. In Greek, it is called *Agape* love. Billy Graham described it this way: "Agape love is supernatural love – no word in any language can describe it."[(14)] Love has no limits. God's love is amazing, it's beautiful, it's all-encompassing, endless and so much more. "And now abide faith, hope, love, these three; but the greatest of these is love" (1 Corinthians 13:13).

For the victim who is no longer a victim but a victor in Christ Jesus, let God be your healer, restorer, repairer, recompense, bridge, living water and life. Let His life be your life; let His light be your light. Let His promises come alive in you. He knows you are fearfully and wonderfully made in His perfect image. We each are our own mold, and the Potter has fashioned each of us in our mold. No two people have the same DNA. We are special and unique, made by our Master Potter, Papa God, and Jesus our vindicator stands by Him, ready to petition for us if the accuser comes accusing. Stand with Jesus Christ. Become one with Him and get to know him. If you let Him, He will definitely direct your paths and ways, and even your thoughts.

Before I end this chapter, I want to address perpetrators of sexual abuse, assault and violence. Some of them are near and dear to my heart because they are very close to me, and it hurts to know this. Just how do you deal with it? How can one address it so as not to be labeled a tale-bearer, snitch or what have you? How can one address it so your family doesn't oust you, stop talking to you, ostracize you, call you all kinds of names? How? I pray that first, you will let God touch your heart and ask Him for forgiveness. Then second, I pray that you will forgive yourself. I pray also that you will be true to yourself and seek the victim of your error and ask for forgiveness. Finally, I pray that you will go after God with all your heart, live life to the fullest and let the past die with the hurt and sins.

Jesus' last words on the cross before He breathed His last were "It Is Finished." It is finished. The work of the cross is finished. He has won the victory for us. Let go and let God. Let Christ minister to your heart and heal you, your family, your children, your job, your marriage, your business, your ministry; let go and let God. Here is a promise that is even for you: "Do not [earnestly] remember the former things; neither consider the things of old. Behold, I am doing a new thing! Now it springs forth; do you not perceive and know it and will you not give heed to it? I will even make a way in the wilderness and rivers in the desert" (Isaiah 43:18-19). God can surely make a way where there is no way. He is God.

The work of the cross of Jesus Christ is complete and finished. It is only our decision that's keeping that promise from being fulfilled. Jesus beckons us to "come to me, all of you who are weary and carry heavy burdens, and I will give you rest" (Matthew 11:28). Choose to rest in Him. Choose to be free! Choose to be whole! Choose to win against the lies of the enemy. Choose to let go! Choose to be healed. Choose life and not death! Choose love. Choose forgiveness. Choose to let God. He is able, available, loving, forgiving, merciful, powerful, mighty, omniscient, omnipotent, omnipresent, all-knowing, ever-present, all-powerful. He is the same yesterday, today and forever! He is the bright and morning star. He is the one true God. He is the living God. He is God.

THE HELPER
Another way to move forward and continue to grow is by living a life led by the Holy Spirit. We are spirit man, and naturally our spirit man will know if something is off or doesn't feel right. That's the spirit within each of us. The Holy Spirit is the spirit of truth (John 16:13). The Bible says He will reveal the truth to you. He will guide you in all things. You don't have to be all holy, no, just be

willing to let Him lead you. He knows all truth. If you lean on Him, you will not be misguided. If you lean on Him, you will be blessed.

LIVING ON PURPOSE

I am spiritually and mentally prepared for the journey ahead, and as this book goes forward I continue to heal and grow in all areas of my life. At first, I felt that I needed to write this book to expose the issue of sexual abuse and sexual assault, and to encourage the women and men affected and lead them to healing. Now, as I write, I can see that this is also a healing process for me, and maybe even closure.

Although marred and almost destroyed by sexual violence, by God's grace and love, I was able to come up for a breath of air. As I struggle and find my way to Him, I have learned so many lessons that have equipped me to help others who may have found themselves in the same place I was in years ago. This is my story, my lesson, my encouragement and my hope for you.

Happiness and peace will come when you find your purpose in life and walk in it. The only way for us to find our purpose is to connect with the Father of all fathers, Lord of all lords, King of all kings, the Prince of peace, the Bright and Morning Star, the Alpha and Omega. Stop the madness and rest in His loving arms. Let Him guide you and nurture you to who you are supposed to be. Break out of the mold, let God break the hard ground of your heart so that it can start healing. Release it to Him. Let go and let God.

Finally, live life to the fullest without shame, without fear, without reservation or anger. Live life now without bitterness, depression or self-harm. I pray that God will be your guide, help and strength as you make your way down the path of healing and restoration. God bless you!

CHAPTER 8
Deliverance & Starting Over

This stench will remain if you don't allow Jesus to remove it from you. It will follow you into your marriage, your career, your job, your life, your ministry, your business – into everything that you do. The turnaround for me began when I was invited to a small church at my first duty location. I didn't realize it then, but I needed God in my life more than ever. It was a season in my life where a lot was happening: within four years, my dad died, I joined the military, my mom had a stroke and my grandmother passed away, and I got married and was expecting a child. I was on an emotional roller coaster. I was 21 years old at that time, and I had not gotten over losing my father. I believe I was still in shock and had not really accepted the fact that my dad was gone. So, for several years, I could not talk about how my dad died. In fact, I really didn't want to talk about it. Whenever I told the story now, it always makes me cry.

While still grieving over the death of my father, I made a major career move and joined the US Army. After a little over a year in the Army, I got pregnant and got married. The day I got married, I was on a plane home – my mom had a stroke, and I was on my way to see her. She was hospitalized the entire three weeks I was home. My mom never fully recovered from the stroke; she had to have someone take care of her 24/7.

Just a couple of months before my mom's stroke, my grandmother, who had told me I was a miracle, passed away. I couldn't attend the funeral, but I really wanted to. At that time, I was clueless as to how the military processes emergency leaves, so I went with what I knew and did what I could do at the moment – just send money home to help out with the funeral expenses. The very next year, I gave birth to my oldest child. My husband and I were also on order to go to Germany. Prior to leaving for Germany, we made plans to go see my mom, but the month before we were supposed to fly home, I got news that she had passed away. At this point, I was now 23, a newlywed and a brand-new mom. These were probably my most trying years, personally, mentally, physically and spiritually. It was during this time that I said "yes" to Christ and began a new journey.

Did it get easy after that? No, definitely not. It was a learning season. The ups and downs with my marriage and my job put me on the edge several times. This was the time when I kept thinking to myself that I was guilty whenever hard times would knock on my door. There was no church that I wanted to attend and plug into, so life went on – the parties, the friends, the alcohol. Life seemed good, but it really wasn't. I was playing my favorite sport and dragging my child with me, leaving my husband home by himself. Balancing marriage, family, work and leisure was not in the picture. Life went on like this for several more years, and then finally, a cousin of mine moved to Germany and we got connected. That connection was heaven-sent, because that was the start of my path back to God. I met her brother and his wife, and they were fired up about Jesus. They were strategically placed in my path to bring me back to the light of Christ.

During our time in Germany, God once again brought people into my life to help me and to make me see that His hand was over me. I had favor in a promotion system that was set against me. My immediate boss didn't want to promote me, and the next higher level supervisor was against it as well. I know I did everything above and beyond my knowledge and abilities for the unit; however, my honesty, outspokenness and integrity were not liked by my immediate superiors. I thank God that His favor got me through that season. I was protected from people who wanted to ruin my career. I was boarded and promoted even when those I worked for directly did not and would not promote me.

A few more years went by, and a few more bumps along the road of life took us to Fort Polk, Louisiana. After three years in Germany, I took my oldest daughter over to my sister back home and went to Virginia for training. My husband and I had signed up for three more years with the Army. We originally had orders for Fort Lewis, Washington, but while we were in training, the Department of the Army decided we weren't going to Washington, but to Fort Polk, Louisiana. That was a setup for what was to come later on that year.

Around the same time, I got pregnant with my second child. The year we arrived in Ft. Polk was the same year Desert Storm operations began, and it was also the year my youngest was born – in fact, she was born the same month things were starting to move that led to Desert Storm. Here I am with a brand-new baby and a four-year-old toddler, and my husband and I are both active duty and were told to get the paperwork for our children together because we will both be deploying. That was a chaotic year. I was running around trying to make sure all the papers were done for my kids and preparing for deployment at the same time. Needless to say, we were also going through post-partum syndrome. But thank God, Ft. Polk did not have to deploy, because the war ended early. After the war, I heard stories of broken marriages and all kinds of craziness that had happened during and after the operation. I was so thankful that we did not deploy. I don't believe my husband and I would still be together today if we had deployed. I'm not saying I would not have done my duty as a soldier, but I was thankful that God kept us back and saved my marriage. Now, on to the next story of my life.

The year after Desert Storm ended, I had an allergic reaction to fire ants that almost killed me. I was due to fly out on a Sunday for temporary duty (TDY) and had to get a physical test (PT) done prior to leaving, so one was scheduled just for me the day before I flew. During my pushups, I was bit on my left hand 21 times by fire ants. Not noticing anything different, other than the sting from the bites, I started on my sit-ups. By the time we were to start the 2-mile run, I had broken out in hives all over my body and I was feeling dizzy. I informed my supervisor and told him I was going to the medical clinic. I didn't even make it to my car – I fainted a few minutes after crossing the street to get to the parking lot. It happened in front of a medical unit barracks – go figure, but God. My pulse had dropped so low it was hard for them to detect it. I had also lost consciousness, but I could still hear. Yes, but God. I was told all this when I regained consciousness. Like I said, I fainted and lost consciousness, and the medics who were forming up for formation ended up working on me until the ambulance arrived to take me to the hospital.

As far as I was aware, I just fainted, and they were taking me to the hospital. I didn't realize that I was now swollen from head to toe and they were trying to get a pulse from me. All I remember is that they kept asking for my name, the day of the week, my birthday, and I was getting agitated because they kept asking the same questions over and over – I later found out that this is what they do to keep the patient conscious. They did not want me to fall asleep and risk never regaining consciousness. I did slip off to a dream or vision of myself in a field of grass and flowers walking towards my girls as they were running towards me. It's funny, but this reminds me of the movie *Gladiator*, when the gladiator is down, and all he sees is his wife and son in a field, and they are walking towards him and him towards them.

I don't know what that dream meant. My thought was that God was telling me that my girls needed me, so it wasn't time for me to go. I was awakened by a bump on the road just before pulling into the emergency area of the hospital. When I finally regained my consciousness and was able to talk to the doctor, I was informed that if I was 15 minutes further down the road then where I was, I would not have survived.

That was a wakeup call for me. I knew I had to get back to church and get back to my word. I had no clue which church to attend, though. I was searching for a church similar to the one I was saved in, so I went looking for one that would teach and preach the Word and speak to the spirit in me. As soon as I was able to find a church, we started having car issues.

If that wasn't bad enough, I was also having issues at work with the leadership because I don't play the game. I've never played the game, especially when I don't think it's the right thing to do. I always speak up, and that has gotten me into difficult situations with the leadership. However, doors have opened to me many times because I stood my ground on the truth and I was trying to do the right thing. I was asked to move ahead of my unit to Fort Hood and establish our office, and I agreed, so my family made the move to Fort Hood. Everything was going well for a minute, but then it was back to the "game" situation again with my outspoken self. For two years, I endured favoritism, discrimination and attempted defamation to my character and career. I fought those fiercely, and I was moved to another unit, thankfully, and worked for a great boss.

This is the point where I also realized that I had to give everything to God – not just some things, but everything. I was tired and frustrated, and I felt like I was always fighting for my life, my career, my marriage, my children, basically everything. It was here where I made peace with God and gave it all to Him. I had done all that I could, but I was still feeling miserable and like I was going around in circles. After making this decision, everything started looking better.

This was the time I was introduced to a beautiful soul, a beautiful young lady who was a friend of my brother and his wife. She watched my children and also invited me to another small church. It was here where I rededicated my life to Christ and made a decision to never go back. When I first started attending, I would sit way in the back, in the last row of chairs, but then God sent a preacher who gave an altar call, and I responded and finally gave it all to Christ. God started moving in my life in miraculous ways, even though the enemy of my soul tried to dissuade me. As in previous years, God was guiding me and showing me His love and favor in everything, only this time, I noticed, and I gladly moved and went as He guided me.

The enemy is vicious and unrelenting. He will not rest until he takes you out or convinces you to take yourself out. But thanks be to God, He never left me nor forsook me. Scripture says that the thief comes not only to steal, kill and to destroy – he will also try and steal your virginity, innocence, sanity, confidence, faith, strength, peace, etc. He will try to destroy you and convince you to do things that will bring self-destruction. I believe living a life opposite to God's original design for me is detrimental to me and my health – mentally, physically, emotionally and spiritually.

Although it was a great time in my life, experiencing a greater zeal for the Lord, serving and hungry for more of His word, His love and His guidance, the enemy continued and was now hitting me closer – attacking the people closest to me. The enemy hates marriage, hates women, hates children, hates man – he hates everyone. Why? Because we are the seed of the woman who will crush his head. He attacked me in my marriage, at my work, with my children, and he continued to try. But now, with a newfound knowledge and wisdom of who God is and what God's Word says, I now know how to combat his schemes.

The only way I was able to maintain peace and find the strength and courage to move forward was by reading the Bible and filling my mind with what the Word of God says: the wisdom in the Psalms, the knowledge of who God is and the love of Christ in the New Testament. This was a process of renewing my mind with the Word of God. All the wrong thinking I had about myself had to be changed. You will only know as much as you are exposed to and allow yourself to be exposed to. Renewing your mind requires a decision, action and consistency. Decide to get well, to believe God's Word, to seek the Word for yourself. God instructs us to study to show ourselves approved unto God (2 Timothy 2:15).

As I mentioned earlier on, I love Joyce Meyer's book *The Battlefield of the Mind*. Before I read her books, I kind of knew the battle between good and evil happened somewhere, but with her teachings, my eyes opened, and I realized how important it is to guard my mind, my eyes, my ears and even my mouth. They're all connected. Once the mind receives a thought, the person has the choice of either ignoring or pondering on that thought. After you ponder on that thought several times, it will eventually go to the heart, and then, "out of the abundance of the heart, the mouth speaks" (Matthew 12:34). God is aware of all of these. Amazing, right? But here I focus on the mind. These quotes from *Battlefield of the Mind* and the Bible emphasize the importance of winning the battle in your mind. That is where the battle really starts. You win the battle by renewing your mind in the Word of God, the Bible.

> Satan takes our circumstances and builds strongholds in our lives—how he wages war on the battlefield of the mind. But, thank God, we have weapons to tear down the strongholds.[8]

> For the weapons of our warfare are not physical [weapons of flesh and blood], but they are mighty before God for the overthrow and destruction of strongholds, [Inasmuch as we] refute arguments and theories and reasonings and every proud and lofty thing that sets itself up against the [true] knowledge of God; and we lead every thought and purpose away captive into the obedience of Christ (the Messiah, the Anointed One). (2 Corinthians 10:4-5)

> God doesn't abandon us and leave us helpless. First Corinthians 10:13 promises us that God will not allow us to be tempted beyond what we can bear, but with every temptation He will also provide the way out, the escape. You may have some major strongholds in your life that need to be broken. Let me encourage you by saying, "God is on your side." There is a war going on, and your mind is the battlefield. But the good news is that God is fighting on your side.[8]

You will guard him and keep him in perfect and constant peace whose mind [both its inclination and its character] is stayed on You, because he commits himself to You, leans on You, *and* hopes confidently in You. (Isaiah 26:3)

The enemy tried to break my marriage up, he tried to harm my youngest and he tried to ruin my career. I must have been on to something for the enemy to attack me in all kinds of ways. I believe when you take that first step towards God and start changing your ways, your word, your life, the enemy is going to come at you with a lot, because he wants to discourage you, he wants you to give up, he wants you to quit, he wants you to take the lower path instead of the high way, he wants you to do it his way and not God's way. But, you see, God's way is not hard – it's actually easy. Jesus said, "Come to me, all of you who are weary and carry heavy burdens, and I will give you rest. Take my yoke upon you. Let me teach you, because I am humble and gentle at heart, and you will find rest for your souls. For my yoke is easy to bear, and the burden I give you is light" (Matthew 11:28-30).

Another turn of events brought me a new sense of direction and newfound hope. My husband retired out of the military, and I was on orders to move to a different state. The military wanted to send me out of the country, but I refused. I was content to sign my exit papers; however, God was not ready for me to leave the military yet. He organized for me to be placed on a wonderful assignment that was the exact opposite of my previous 11 years in the military. Although my family did not accompany me, the next two years proved to be yet another test and another way God was showing me who He really was in my life. God provided for me and my family even in the toughest financial time of our lives. In that time, we had to face the test of depending completely and totally on God's financial plan. For two years, we managed, and I was struggling to stay faithful to God's plan for financial sufficiency, but I realized later that it was the best way. There is no better way than God's way. From then on, I stuck to God's plan and never wavered again. Now my faith has grown, and I trust God to meet our needs.

By God's grace, I was able to return to the same location where my family was. In the following years, God placed me in a unit where I would have favor with the leaders. I was promoted and sent to advance schooling, and then I was offered a leadership position with another unit. I accepted, and two years later, I had orders to go to South Korea. Here, once again, God showed up and showed out. He was always a few steps ahead of me. Although I was given scary talks of being assigned close to the border between North and South Korea, I told God that wherever He leads me, I know I will be all right because He's my daddy. However, out of the blue, I got assigned to a unit in Seoul, South Korea. Everyone in my field thought I had connections with people at the Department of the Army and somehow finagled my way to this assignment, but none of that happened. I just trusted God to lead me where He saw fit. All I could do was laugh and thank God for looking after me.

Remember the story of Abraham's servant, sent on a mission to find a suitable wife for Isaac. The servant just prayed and trusted God to lead him and to lead Rebecca to him. Of course, the story went just as the servant had requested of God – chosen by God and orchestrated by God. Isn't that amazing? I serve an amazing God and Father, and you can have the same thing.

I returned to the States a year later, to my family and to the unit I wanted to go back to. Two years after that, as I was preparing myself to exit the military once again, I had orders ready and was making plans for what I would do once I got out, but upon returning from the funeral of one of my uncles, I was told that I was deploying and the unit wouldn't let me retire because they needed me.

This is the turning point where not only was God preparing me for ministry, but He was purging me of any bitterness and any hard-heart issues that may hinder me from fulfilling the ministry He has for me. In 2004, I deployed with my unit to Iraq. It was the same year my oldest was graduating from high school, and the only thing I wanted to do was to be able to return for my daughter's graduation. It was an unpredictable time, and Operation Iraqi Freedom had just started the year before. I was told there was no guarantee I would be able to return for the graduation, but I kept reminding God that He's Abba, and that I wanted to be back to attend that event. My fellow associate even teased me and made jokes that I wouldn't be able to leave. I told him that he doesn't know who my Father is, and just watch, I will be going home for my daughter's graduation. And I did. It was also during this time that I encountered some serious women's health issues. But at the same time, I was determined to seek God more.

I attended church every Sunday, attended a prayer meeting at lunch on weekdays and Saturdays and attended Bible studies several times a week. There, God trained me for prayer and increased my knowledge of the Word. I had seen others take the opposite direction, saying "What happens in Iraq stays in Iraq." I never liked that saying, even when I would hear it said about National Training Center or South Korea.

Iraq is also where I opened up to a sister about the sexual assault I experienced when I was a little girl. When I did that, it felt good. It gave me strength and courage to maybe share it with others as the opportunity presents itself. This was the beginning of a sharing process that led to conversations with others and with some of my nieces. It led me to the knowledge that there must be something that can be done to help counter the effects of this barbaric and cowardly act.

How did I overcome the stench of this incident? When I was attending one of the local churches, there was a women's retreat they hosted every year. The first time I went, I was blown away by how good it was, and it helped move my healing process further along. There were classes for help in areas such as marriage, parenting, business and so on. At the end of the retreat on our last night, we gathered in the big room for worship service and prayer. This was the first time someone prayed about the sexual abuse in my life. Every time I went after that, I would stand when they prayed for those who had experienced sexual abuse, and each time, it felt better. I then started praying for the others at the same meeting, and by that point, I was also praying for others for salvation and other needs at the church.

This was truly a turning point in my life. Over the next ten years, I continued to pray for others, read and learn from the Word of God, and learn from other pastors, evangelists, ministers, and preachers, including my own pastor. As I worked and helped out in ministries, I continued to grow in my faith. There were times when I held Bible study in my home, thanks to the help and encouragement of one of my spiritual daughters. It then expanded to the women in the church, but that didn't last long. Why is it so difficult for women in the church to come together and just pray – to lighten the chatter, and pray and speak life more?

In 2013, I was invited to a prayer meeting by a good pastor friend of mine. Little did I know that I would be starting a prayer group a year later. God actually dropped a desire in my heart to gather the pastors' wives in a prayer meeting to pray for the local churches, especially the Samoan churches. There was so much animosity and division, and it didn't sit right in my spirit. So, with the alignment and agreement of two of the sisters, Women of Purpose was birthed. Today, Women of Purpose is not only a prayer group, but a group with a purpose to pray for women and affect women's lives for the better.

BE SET FREE

With young girls, women or men who are living a lifestyle contrary to God's original intent, I know it's their choice, but I wonder if that lifestyle has really set them free. I believe that as long as they are living that lifestyle, they are denying the fact that God is able to restore and redeem the time for them and their life. God is much more capable and willing to help if we let Him. If you're a girl who is living a life of homosexuality, I encourage you to read the Word and put your ear close to God's heart. That lifestyle is so contrary to what God intended for you to live. It's a life built on lies, deceit, false ideas, pride and false dreams. We are created in God's image.

He is God, and He designed and weaved your DNA to make you a girl. You are not only designed but purposed to be a girl. In Jeremiah 1:5 God the Father said, "I knew you before I formed you in your mother's womb." Isn't that something? He already knew you were going to be born – the time, day and hour. He even said, "Before you were born I set you apart." What a loving Father we have. He loves you just as much as He loves me. Seek your "set apart" role and destiny, and when you find it, walk in it and experience the supernatural nature and power of God in your life.

As with any life decisions, so it is with God. It is just a decision to step out or up and let God restore, renew and completely set you free of that bondage – and it is bondage. It is bondage of lies, deceit, pretense, hurt, unforgiveness, pride, and the list can go on. I am confident that there is more for you than this. God is a loving God, and He wants the best for you, for me, for all of us.

OVERCOME AND CONQUER
At one time, I didn't care about who I was with, but as time went by, I realized that I didn't want any disease, I didn't want a child out of wedlock, I didn't want anyone who would physically abuse me and I definitely didn't want anyone to treat me like a street woman – a hooker. I experienced all these in my first few years in the military. I was quickly learning more and more about the nature of men and women alike, and I started to separate myself from these groups of people. Then I met and fell in love with the love of my life, who is now my husband, and we had two beautiful children. Along that journey were other learning experiences that I have had to conquer and overcome. It seemed that every stage in my life was a new challenge and a growth spurt.

It's going to be the same for you, but it will get better. We use those experiences and release them so that others can learn from them and not suffer from making the same mistake. I had to learn and overcome in order to conquer each hurdle. When I accepted Christ as my Savior, I began another journey through another hurdle. Every turn and every direction you take will have hurdles, and through those hurdles is a learning experience. You must overcome and conquer it, or it will overtake you and turn into a vicious and unpleasant cycle that will repeat itself over and over.

PREGNANT OUT OF WEDLOCK – MY SAVIOR

I got engaged to my husband, but before we got married, I got pregnant. God's grace is so wide and high, you cannot hide or run away from it. It was during this time that I accepted Christ into my heart as my Lord and Savior in the early part of 1986, just before the birth of my firstborn child. God brought members of my own family into my life who would lead me to church and introduce me to Jesus Christ the Savior. Now, I know some of you reading this might think, "Well, who did you know when you were going to church all these years?" I knew of God and reverenced Him, but I did not have a personal relationship with Christ, the Son of God. There is a difference. However, God knew all this and incorporated all these experiences in my life to bring me to this point.

DESERT STORMS

At times, we have to go through a desert for God to bring our attention back to Him. As for me, when I went through my desert, I started seeking Him out again. Sometimes, I had to leave my house and go to church to get a word. I was not reading my Bible and hardly praying. It's funny how when you hit some rough patches in life, that's when you quickly remember God. That's what He does – He lets you hit the rough spot so you can look up and seek Him. Things are much easier, less painful and clearer when you connect to Him.

Even though I had been so-called "saved" and baptized in water, I backslid. Even though my husband was a chaplain assistant at that time, that didn't help things. I had to seek God out for myself. Things were happening left and right with our cars, our marriage and my family. It was a crazy time – a time when I almost lost my life to fire ant bites, got into a car accident, gave birth to my second child and was having challenges at work with the leadership. But God was there to meet me halfway.

GOD BY YOUR SIDE

My path to the Father became clearer when, at age nine, I took a liking to a radio program called Children's Bible Hour. Another thing in my childhood that led me down the path to Jesus Christ was listening to Jimmy Swaggart's cassette tapes with my cousin and very close friend Tele. We loved the music, and we would listen to those songs over and over again. I also remember watching the Oral Roberts program on TV every Sunday morning. It came on at eight and finished at nine, the time when I should be in church. I enjoyed those programs. I was curious and fascinated by the word, the worship and the miracles.

In my adult life, God brought help – my angels in disguise. Some were family or friends of my family, and others were strangers. As we moved around in the military, we would encounter families who would redirect me to the Father's house (the church). He sent an angel to help me at work. He sent angels to help us with our children. He sent angels to help me find my way back to church. He sent angels to help me and strengthen me to keep me calm in my marriage. So, during our next move, God met us there once again. We were able to find great sitters for our children and eventually come back to God's house.

THE ENEMY OF MY SOUL, MY FAMILY

In that same year of our move from Louisiana to Texas, we almost lost our youngest daughter, who was only two years old, but thank God for His angels who directed her to my sitter's house. Only God could have protected her. That was the beginning of the end to a long and dry drought for me, my husband and my family, although it was close for me – that same year, I lost one of my sisters. In those times, I was just going. There was no direction, and there seemed to be walls everywhere I turned. But then I was invited to church by my children's sitter. That was the start of a beautiful journey that would bring me to who I am today. This time, I knew what I needed to do, and I was now fully on board with what God wanted to do through me. I had so much more to learn, but as I pursued God, He directed me through the maze of life.

I remember when my grandmother told me that I was special. I asked her why, and she told me it was because I could have died in my mother's womb, but I was spared and entered life unmaimed by the incident that could have taken both my and my mom's lives. I was a teenager when we had this conversation, I believe in high school. I asked my mom, and she confirmed the story. It was during a storm; she was pinned under a tree and she was due to have me within days. Praise God for His protection and for His direction. Praise God for His grace, mercy and undying and unmerited favor. Praise God for His unconditional love. Praise God for life and for a blessed life. Thank you, Father!

My God is my guide and vindicator. "Though an army may encamp against me, my heart shall not fear; though war may rise against me, in this I *will be* confident" (Psalm 27:3). These scriptures strengthen me and let me know that God's got my back. I stand tall and walk tall, for my God will save me and protect me. I'm not arrogant, just sure and confident in my God. The God of the universe, Jehovah God, the Almighty, loves each and every one of us, whether male or female; we are all made in His image. He wants the best for each of us. "'For I know the plans I have for you,' says the Lord. 'They are plans for good and not for disaster, to give you a future and a hope'" (Jeremiah 29:11). What a loving God we have.

HELP IS HERE
Help will come, and it will come when you seek and desire it. Is it from friends, family, other people, the government? Perhaps so – we have a loving Father, and He will bring people into your life and path to help guide you along. Our job and responsibility is to recognize it, step out in faith and do the work, taking courage to step forth and just do it. The fruit will come if you're faithful. This is a natural law with the Father. It is His promise. He will not go back on what He has spoken. The greatest and most lasting help will come from God the Father through His Son Jesus. We are born into this world as sinners, but as we come face to face with Christ and let Him be our true Savior, life takes on a different facet. We

are made new in Christ, and it is not I who live but Christ that lives in me. He is the Savior who came to take away the sin of the world so that through Him we may have eternal life and our sins forgiven.

It is time to wage war against this evil, this plague, this lie of the enemy. For far too long, children, women and men have fallen victim to these lies, these behaviors and these iniquities. We cannot completely eradicate it, but we can sure blacken its eye and bring it down, minimize its effects and destroy its ways of causing havoc now and in the future for everyone, especially the children and women. The promises of God are so amazing, and they are for you and me; however, He will not force them on you. He has given each of us a will, and that willpower is what we as His creation must exercise to accept or refuse the help, and most importantly, the promise He has spoken and given for us. How would you find out and know about all these promises? It's really simple. Decide to receive the knowledge and revelation of God's Word for yourself by reading and studying His Word. The Holy Spirit whom God has sent to help you and me will help you understand the nature of God and His love for you. He is the Spirit of Truth, and He will reveal to you exactly what God's will is for you.

In the end, I had to forgive myself first, and then I had to forgive the perpetrator. In fact, I had to forgive everyone I may have blamed for what had happened to me, and most importantly, I had to share my story. I had to give it to God and trust Him completely. I had to make and allow time for healing. I received my healing through the retreats, sermons, teachings and prayer I received. In order for anyone to be healed, all these things have to be received. I had to renew my mind with God's Word. I had to learn to speak life and not death. I had to decide to walk in victory for the rest of my life by standing firm in my convictions and by telling the truth.

Lastly, but most importantly, I had to let the love of God rule in my life. I couldn't have done it if the love of God was not in my heart. God is love. The ultimate evidence of His love was shown through His Son Jesus. "For this is how God loved the world: He gave his one and only Son, so that everyone who believes in him will not perish but have eternal life" (John 3:16). This is not the final destination – eternity is. I would rather spend it in Heaven where there is no more tears, pain or death. Hell is much worse (Revelation 21; Matthew 8:12, 13:42, 22:13, 24:51, 25:30; Luke 13:28).

GROW AND BLOOM AS HE WATERS

To sum up my thoughts and heart in this writing, I want to share these great thoughts and wisdom from Napoleon Hill in his *Think and Grow Rich* book. "Happiness is found in doing, not merely possessing."[20] "Every adversity, every failure, every heartbreak, carries with it the seed of an equal or greater benefit."[20] "If you do not conquer self, you will be conquered by self."[20]

Finally, one of the greatest stories ever told, the story of this young woman who defied the fact that she was deaf and blind: "Helen Keller became deaf, dumb, and blind shortly after birth. Despite her greatest misfortune, she has written her name indelibly in the pages of the history of the great. Her entire life has served as evidence that *no one is ever defeated until defeat has been accepted as reality.*"[20]

Although I made a decision to join the military on a whim of an emotional context, by God's grace, it turned out to be the best decision I ever made. God is so loving, even when you take the wrong turn, He lovingly brings you back to where you need to be. I believe it was my destiny. It took me a long time to get to that understanding, but I eventually did. Praise God.

There are times when I felt that what happened to me was because I sinned or had done something wrong. However, I realized later that it wasn't anything I did. I found courage in this scripture: "There is therefore now no condemnation to those who are in Christ Jesus" (Romans 8:1). I now know I am a child of God, and that is His promise for me. I received it and rejoice in the freedom that it has given me. What that means is, even if I did something wrong, if I recognize and accept my error and I ask God to forgive me, God will forgive me and will forget all of my sins. "As far as the east is from the west, so far has He removed our transgressions from us" (Psalm 103:12). I also know and believe that the sting of death has been removed from me (1 Corinthians 15:54-58). Hallelujah and amen! Praise be to God who was, and is, and is to come!

The beginning was rough, stained, full of hurt and disappointments. But, praise God for His faithfulness, love and mercy, I have overcome them all. I have been restored, renewed, made whole, and I live because Jesus lives. I am victorious because Jesus gained the victory for me. I have overcome because Christ paid the price for my sins and my shortcomings and has given me a new heart to forgive and let my enemies go.

Through one's journey, seeds are planted along the way. These seeds were planted by God to guide you along the way to His heart, and they are forgiveness, mercy and love. When they bloom, they will bloom into the fruits of the Spirit: love, joy, peace, patience, kindness, goodness, faithfulness, gentleness and self-control (Galatians 5:23). These are evident in all goodness, righteousness and truth (Ephesians 5:9). You see, we were born into sin. We didn't know any better, but along the way, we start learning. God planted seeds through your parents. He planted seeds through your friends and family. He planted seeds through your trials and your victories. He planted seeds through the church, through your education, through your children, through your job and your co-workers. He planted seeds everywhere. Because He planted those seeds in my life, the blooms from those seeds were my guide to Him. In every adversity, there was a teaching, a light breaking through the horizon, a flower blooming in the midst of weeds, a small reminder that God was right there, guiding, watching and directing me.

I love how Joyce Meyer explains our minds:

> When the battle seems endless and you think you'll never make it, remember that you are reprogramming a very carnal, fleshly, worldly mind to think as God thinks. Impossible? No! Difficult? Yes! But, just think, you have God on your team. I believe He is the best "computer

programmer" around. (Your mind is like a computer that has had a lifetime of garbage programmed into it.) God is working on you; at least, He is if you have invited Him to have control of your thoughts. He is reprogramming your mind. Just keep cooperating with Him—and *don't give up!* Satan will aggressively fight against the renewal of your mind, but it is vital that you press on and continue to pray and study in this area until you gain measurable victory.[8]

Amen and amen!

Now, with the knowledge and understanding I have about this crippling and devastating devil, surrendering my life to my Lord and letting Him change and heal me, I am set free and forever grateful and blessed. Now it's your turn. It is time for you to take that step of faith and move forward to your purpose, to the destiny that God has mapped out for you. It is time to muster up the courage and take action. It's your season, and it's my season too. It is our season to rise, to come out, to shout for joy, for the Lord is good and He is faithful. It's time to be free. It is time to be set free. It is time to move. It is time to make a difference, to make a change for you, for your children, for your family, for your friends, for everyone.

It is time to speak up!

Songs for the Soul and Spirit

These are some of the songs that have been keys in my spiritual and victory walk daily. These songs encouraged my spirit-man; they have helped me reconnect to my Lord. They have helped build up my courage, strength, faith and resolve. "The Lord is my strength and my shield; my heart trusted in Him, and I am helped; therefore my heart greatly rejoices, and with my song I will praise Him" (Psalm 28:7).

- This Little Light of Mine

- There is a River

- I Never Lost My Praise (*Brooklyn Tabernacle Choir*)

- You Know My Name (*Tasha Cobbs Leonard*)

- Victory Belongs to Jesus (*Todd Dulaney*)

- Way Maker (*Sinach*)

- You Are My Strength (*William Murphy*)

- God I Look to You (*Tasha Cobbs Leonard*)

Nafanua Manns

Prayers

PRAYER OF SALVATION

Father, I know I'm a sinner. Please forgive me and take away my sins. Jesus, I believe you died and rose again from the dead, and now you are sitting on the right hand of God. I make you the Lord of my life. Come into my heart. Come live in me and through me. Thank you for saving me. Help me and guide me from this point on. Have your way in my life, Jesus. In Jesus' name I ask, amen.

"Whoever calls on the name of the Lord shall be saved" (Acts 2:21). "If you confess with your mouth the Lord Jesus and believe in your heart that God has raised Him from the dead, you will be saved"(Romans 10:9).

PRAYER FOR THE VICTIM AFTER SALVATION

Father, your word that you send out does not return to you without accomplishing what it was sent out to do. In accordance with your word, Father, if I ask, it will be given to me, if I seek, I will find and if I knock, the door will be opened to me. Today I ask that you remove any stain of shame, low self-esteem, depression, discouragement, unworthiness, fear of rejection and failure far from me. Father, open my eyes and expel all the lies of the enemy from me that have kept me prisoner for so long. Father, give me a renewed mind, heal my heart and my soul. Give me the wisdom, knowledge, courage and strength to walk the path that you have designed for me. Thank you, Father, that the path is clear to me, and I can see it with spiritual eyes. The enemy no longer has a hold on me. He is a defeated foe, and he is under my feet. Christ has won the victory for me, and "it is finished!" Help me as I walk the walk of forgiveness for the perpetrator. Thank you, Father, for the deliverance, the victory and the freedom I have found in you. I praise you and honor you and give you all the glory. In Jesus' name I ask and I thank you, amen!

PRAYER FOR THE PERPETRATOR AFTER THE PRAYER OF SALVATION

Father God, you are the Lord of all. I ask you to give me the wisdom, courage and strength to move forward. Father, guide and direct me in the way I should go. Shine the light of your love in the path I need to take to forgiveness and restoration. Father God, I will stand on Romans 8:1 which says, "therefore, [there is] now no condemnation (no adjudging guilty of wrong) for those who are in Christ Jesus, who live [and] walk not after the dictates of the flesh, but after the dictates of the Spirit. Thank you Father. In Jesus name, amen.

Personal Affirmations

I am fearfully and wonderfully made. I am the apple of God's eye. I am forgiven, renewed, restored and cleansed by the Blood of the Lamb who is Jesus Christ. I am blessed and highly favored. I am the head and not the tail, above only and not beneath. No weapon formed against me shall prosper. The enemy may come at me one way but flee out seven ways. I am blessed going out and blessed coming in. I am blessed in the field and in the city. The fruit of my womb is blessed. My job is blessed. My bank account is blessed. My business is blessed. My ministry is blessed. My family is blessed. My household is blessed. The increase in my physical body, spirit and soul are blessed.

My children are blessed. They are taught by God, and great shall be their peace. My children are walking in accordance to their God-given destiny and purpose. They receive favor everywhere they go, in everything they touch and everything they do. No harm will come to them. Their minds are protected, as well as their spirit and soul, from the influence of the enemy. Their eyes are wide open to see your truth, Father, in accordance to your Word and what the Holy Spirit reveals to them. In Jesus' mighty name, amen.

Nafanua Manns

References

1. Eleanor Ainge Roy, "'The silence is suffocating': family abuse 'epidemic' uncovered in Samoa," The Guardian, 2019. https://www.theguardian.com/global-development/2019/sep/03/family-abuse-epidemic-uncovered-in-samoa

2. Centers for Disease Control and Prevention, "Sexual Violence is Preventable."https://www.cdc.gov/injury/features/sexual-violence/

3. Asian Pacific Institute on Gender-Based Violence, "Fact Sheet: Pacific Islanders and Domestic & Sexual Violence, 2018."https://www.api-gbv.org/resources/dvfactsheet-pacificislander/

4. Australian Institute of Health and Welfare (AIHW),"Family, domestic and sexual violence in Australia: continuing the national story,"2019.https://www.aihw.gov.au/reports/domestic-violence/family-domestic-sexual-violence-australia-2019/contents/table-of-contents

5. United Nations Population Fund (UNFPA), "Women Who Experience Intimate Partner Violence, 2000-2017: UNFPA Asia and the Pacific Region," 2017.

6. Rape, Abuse & Incest National Network (RAINN).https://www.rainn.org/about-rainn

7. L.R. Penland, "Sex Education in 1900, 1940 and 1980: An Historical Sketch," 1981. https://pubmed.ncbi.nlm.nih.gov/7015007

8. Joyce Meyer, Battlefield of the Mind: Winning the Battle in Your Mind, 1995.

9. American Psychological Association (APA).https://www.apa.org

10. US Department of Justice.https://www.justice.gov

11. National Sexual Violence Resource Center.https://www.nsvrc. org/statistics

12. Rape Crisis,"About Sexual Violence: Myths about rape and sexual violence."https://rapecrisis.org.uk/get-informed/about-sexual-violence/myths-vs-realities/

13. Trinity College, "Curriculum Changes of Sex Education Through The Years," 2016. https://commons.trincoll.edu/edreform/2016/05/curriculum-changes-of-sex-education-through-the-years/

14. Billy Graham, True Love(Billy Graham Classic).

15. Violence Against Women Network, "Pornography and Sexual Violence," 2004.https://vawnet.org/material/pornography-and-sexual-violence

16. Shane James O'Neill, "Sexual abuse and pornography," 2020. https://www.provenmen.org/sexual-abuse-and-pornography/

17. Resilience: Empowering survivors, Ending sexual violence, "Effects of Sexual Violence." https://www.ourresilience.org/

18. Love Is Respect blog, "Love is Setting Boundaries: What Are My Boundaries?" 2016.https://www.loveisrespect.org/content/what-are-my-boundaries/

19. Dr. Henry Cloud and Dr. John Townsend,Boundaries: When to Say Yes, How to Say No to Take Control of Your Life, 1992.www. boundariesbooks.com

20. Napoleon Hill, Think and Grow Rich, 1937.

21. Sam Carr, "How pornography removes empathy – and fosters harassment and abuse," The Conversation, 2017. https:// theconversation.com/how-pornography-removes-empathy-and-fosters-harassment-and-abuse-86643

SCRIPTURES QUOTED FROM:
- NLT – New Living Translation

- NKJV –New King James Version

- AMP – Amplified Bible

Nafanua Manns

Resources

- Office of Violence Against Women (OVW)
  https://www.justice.gov/ovw

- Rape, Abuse & Incest National Network (RAINN)
  National Sexual Assault Hotline: 1-800-656-HOPE
  24/7 Advocates Available (Chat)
  https://hotline.rainn.org/online
  https://www.rainn.org/about-rainn

- National Center for Victims of Crime
  1-855-4-VICTIM (855-484-2846)

- National Institute of Justice, https://nij.ojp.gov

- Centers of Disease Control and Prevention (CDC), https://www.cdc.gov

- Office on Women's Health, https:www.womenhealth.gov/office-womens-health

- National Resource Center on Domestic Violence
  (NRCDV)
  https://www.nrcdv.org/

- US Violence Against Women Act (VAWA)
  Violence Against Women network (VAWnet)
  https://vawnet.org/about

- Anastasia Powell,"Rape culture: why our community attitudes to sexual violence matter," The Conversation, 2014.https://theconversation.com/rape-culture-why-our-community-attitudes-to-sexual-violence-matter-31750

NON-PROFIT ORGANIZATIONS
- American Samoa:
  Alliance Against Domestic and Sexual Violence
  PO Box 4459, Pago Pago, American Samoa 96799
  Phone: (684) 699-0272
  http://www.asalliance.co/

- ICAN Window of Hope (Fa'amalama o le Fa'amoemoe)
  Fa'aalu Leva'a F. Iuli (Alu)
  icanwindowofhope@gmail.com
  www.ican-window-of-hope-85.webself.net
  American Samoa: 1 (684) 258-5959
  Australia: 00 61 (435) 176-869
  Seattle, US: (808) 232-8340

- PIK2AR – Pacific Island Knowledge 2 Action Resources
  Susi Feltch-Malohifo'ou
  Executive Director
  US Mainland (801) 793-4639
  susi@pik2ar.org

- Women of Purpose Grp (WOP)
  Nafanua F. Manns (Nua) CEO & Founder
  US Mainland: (254) 415-4270
  nua.wopgrp2014@gmail.com

FACEBOOK SPACES TO MEET AND SHARE
- Women's EmpowHERment Group:
  Susi Feltch-Malohifo'ou

- WOP-GRP & WOH Partnership
  Faaalu Leva'a F Iuli (Alu)
  Juliet Parker
  Nafanua F Manns (Nua)

Made in the USA
Columbia, SC
12 October 2020